RIDERS UNLOCK YOUR RIDING SUCCESS

THE ULTIMATE GUIDE FOR RIDERS AND THEIR SUPPORT TEAM

CLAIRE NIXON-ORD UKCC LEVEL 4 COACH
TRACEY COLE BSC, PHD

AND CO.

CONTENTS

FOREWORD

We are grateful to everyone who has been part of our own equestrian journeys. It has been a pleasure working together on this book together with coaches and riders from an array of disciplines and levels.

We'd like to say a big thank you to all the unsung heroes – those who help to support riders, who celebrate the victories and listen to their woes, who travel to lessons, clinics and competitions and spend their weekends watching their ridings and willing them on to do well! You were the inspiration for this book.

We also want to thank you the reader, this book is to help anyone who is interested in improving their horse riding and horsemanship and to help the support crew so that they know how best to champion their rider. We want this book to help and guide riders into becoming the rider they wish to become.

We have divided this book into three sections. The first is all about you, the second is about the rider and the last section deals with the rider's supporter. It's important to read all the sections, no matter your perspective, to have the very best understanding.

We are so pleased to be part of your riding journey, remember to ask for help, there is no such thing as a stupid question. We'd love to hear from you if you have any comments or questions.

With sincere gratitude,

Claire and Tracey

X

ARE YOU IN THE RIGHT SPACE?

Before you dig into this book, we want to make sure you are in the right place to begin.

Rider's Minds have a great rider checker to make sure you are in the right space.

Please visit:

https://ridersminds.org/my-mental-health-checker/ to ensure you are ready to begin.

If you have any thoughts or worries there are people who are out there to help.

FOR ADULTS:

Call NHS 111 (for when you need help but are not in immediate danger)

Contact your GP and ask for an emergency appointment.

Contact the Samaritans at www.samaritans.org

116 123 (free to call from within the UK and Ireland), 24 hours a day

Use the 'Shout' crisis text line - text SHOUT to 85258

https://ridersminds.org/get-support/i-need-help/

RIDER'S MINDS SUPPORT LINES

Our 24-hour, 7 days a-week services, mean that you are never alone and there is always a trained helper ready to talk to you.

The helpline, text and chat lines are for you if you are having challenges within the workplace or life in general, for example bullying, or are feeling low and unhappy.

We offer callers confidential help on a range of mental health and well-being issues.

Call: 0300 102 1540

Or if you prefer to message then text: 07860 065 202

www.mind.org.uk **Info Line: 0300 123 3393 to call, or text 86463** Email info@mind.org.uk

YOUNG PEOPLE AND CHILDREN:

Rider's Minds Support lines

Our 24-hour, 7 days a week services, mean that you are never alone and there is always a trained helper ready to talk to you.

The helpline, text and chat lines are for you if you are having challenges within the workplace or life in general, for example, bullying, or are feeling low and unhappy.

We offer callers confidential help on a range of mental health and well-being issues.

Call: 0300 102 1540

Or if you prefer to message then text: 07860 065 202

www.youngminds.org.uk

Parents helpline: 0808 802 5544 (Mon-Fri from 9.30am to 4pm, excluding bank holidays)

Young Minds Crisis Messenger: text YM to 85258 (available 24/7)

https://www.mind.org.uk/for-young-people/how-to-get-help-and-support/useful-contacts/

PART I

YOU

In this section, you'll start to understand yourself and how your mind works

1

YOUR 7-YEAR-OLD SELF: YOUR VALUES AND BELIEFS

Have you ever had someone give you advice that you know wouldn't work for you? Maybe the advice was sound, but it didn't feel right to you. It wouldn't be the way you would go about it, yet it works for others.

How our mind filters out what we want, believe and find important, is as individual as a fingerprint. What's not immediately obvious is that we often suppose that we way in which others filter is the same (or very close) to our way.

For example, how are you choosing to read this book? Did you look at the content's page first, did you read the back cover, read the section that applied most to you, skim-read some pages or simply start here, in the first chapter? There's no right or wrong is there? But we make a choice based on our beliefs about the book, what's of value to us and our preference about reading style.

Now imagine we have beliefs, values and preferences in our coaching and coachee styles. We would coach in a certain manner and would like to be coached in a certain manner. It's a personal preference. Knowing yourself and your filters is empowering. It keeps you focused and enables you to gain and maintain motivation and resilience. Knowing someone else's preferred way of thinking and behaving gives you more depth and breadth and enhances your support of a rider.

All of our beliefs, values and preferences are part of the neuroplasticity of our minds; that means we can change how we think and behave when one of these filters no longer serves us. To understand better how we develop these filters; we can delve a little into the various phases of their development.

MASSEY'S PERIODS OF DEVELOPMENT

0-7 YEARS OLD – THE IMPRINT PERIOD

In this time, our experiences are viewed through the prism of innocence and sometimes vulnerable eyes. This is a time when we imprint those around us; we copy without question. We are very sensitive sponges, able to absorb others' beliefs, values and preferences. What we experience here is often a blueprint for later life. We subconsciously begin to establish behaviours that mimic others.

7-14 YEARS OLD – THE MODELLING PERIOD

Here we begin to be impressed by people of our choosing, rather than the passive absorption of the previous ages. We model 'heroes', be they people we know or people who influence us. We try opinions on like clothes but are ready to discard them later on.

A certain level of responsibility is felt and life can be perceived as unfair, especially during puberty when emotions are charged with hormones. In fact, immense physical, emotional and mental changes occur. In this confusing and relatively chaotic period, adolescents often misinterpret others' emotions and are far more impulsive than at other times which can give rise to problems[1].

There may be a time of withdrawal, like a butterfly larva changing into a chrysalis.

[1]Neuropsychiatr Dis Treat. 2013; 9: 449–461. **Maturation of the adolescent brain.** Mariam Arain, Maliha Haque, Lina Johal, Puja Mathur, Wynand Nel, Afsha Rais, Ranbir Sandhu, and Sushil Sharma. Published online 2013 Apr 3.

14-21 YEARS OLD – SOCIALISATION PERIOD

The chrysalis will withdraw and then develop into a butterfly. Young people in this category will be most impacted by their peers' thoughts, values and behaviours. Ideas about relationships with others begin to take shape and from the age of 14, we are developing a sense of self that may require time away –

university, travelling, a job – that allows them to become the butterfly.

OUR BELIEFS, VALUES AND PREFERENCES

Beliefs, values and preferences are moulded throughout these developmental time periods. Some of the deepest and most locked-in core beliefs, values and preferences are generated in the imprint period of 0-7 years old. That isn't to say that they are disadvantageous to us, more that they can be very much outside of our awareness, in spite of providing a framework on which we place our motivation, hopes, dreams and go-to emotions.

FINDING YOUR OWN BELIEFS, VALUES AND PREFERENCES

1. YOUR BELIEFS

Beliefs develop once our unconscious mind has accumulated enough of what it accepts as evidence to support that belief. Before we take on a belief, there is a decision point, where the mind asks, 'Do I have enough evidence to believe this?' If there is enough evidence, the belief will be created.

What then is the evidence? Very often, when we analyse a self-limiting belief, the evidence is either flimsy, unreliable or made when our mind was sensitive and/or vulnerable. Armed with this knowledge, we can poke a stick around a limiting belief to loosen it and be on our way to eliminating it.

We're going to find out what you believe about yourself as a person, as a rider and what you believe about your riding ability. Here is a series of prompts to help you.

(a)   How would a good friend describe you? Give as many descriptions as you want – go for at least 10!

(b)   Looking at your descriptions from the previous question, which ones do you *really believe* to be true?

(c)   Looking at your list from the previous question, aren't you so much more than that? Give at least 3 other descriptions that you believe about yourself.

(d)   Repeat Questions 1-3 for you as a rider.

(e)   Do you have self-limiting beliefs? What are they? (Limiting beliefs will seem very real and true to you; other people may not agree with these and find that you are good enough, talented enough, deserving enough etc.)

(f)   How specifically do these self-limiting beliefs stop you from obtaining your goals?

(g)   When specifically do these self-limiting beliefs stop you from obtaining your goals?

(h)   When did you develop this belief?

If you don't know the answers to any of the questions, give yourself a quiet moment to journal on this. Simply write using pen and paper to slow down your thoughts and pour onto the page everything you know about this belief – how it feels, how it makes you think, what mind's eye pictures it

17

gives you. Then, when you have a very full description, acknowledge where the belief may have sprung from. Was there a particular event, did somebody say something to you or were you taught to believe this by someone else?

Now, having the intention to get rid of a limiting belief is the first step, taking action is the second. Journal on what action to take. This is perhaps the most important part. Don't skip this! Allow ideas to flow, without forcing them. If you are reminded of a memory or you see something in your mind's eye, write it down. The meaning will become apparent as you write or later.

Knowing that a limiting belief may not even have started as your own belief, but rather that it was something that was passed on to you, can help to loosen its power over you.

Here are more questions to consider to help you to break down a limiting belief. Refer to these questions often and journal on them to give even more insight.

(a) Will this belief help or hurt me?

(b) Is this belief motivating me or de-motivating me?

(c) What do I want people to believe about me? This tells us what you really want or need to believe about yourself

(d) Is this belief moving me closer to my goals and aspirations or taking me further away?

2. YOUR VALUES

Values are those things that we find important. We can have values that we don't like, but we know that it's important. Values can be obvious and within easy reach of our conscious mind (family, friends, horses, riding etc.). Values can be very much deeper and more abstract (love, harmony, freedom etc.).

(a)   Write down 20 values (or more) that you have at this moment – these are not aspirational values.

Now we're going to add even more values to your list. The feeling you get just before you're motivated to do something is another value. Think about a specific time when you were really motivated in life to do something. Just before you got up and did it, how did you feel? Repeat for another 2-3 specific memories of being intensely motivated.

(b)   Add all these emotions to your values list.

(c)   Looking down your list of values, choose your top 8, in any order.

(d)   Now rank them 1-8, with number 1 being the most important to you.

(e)   Consider your list. Have you really included everything you would want in life? In riding? Success, motivation, joy – would you want these added and where in your list of 8 would be best to insert them?

(f)   Is anything else missing?

Your mind will be driven by and willing to expend lots of energy and effort on value no.1.

Your mind will put effort and energy into number 2.

Your mind will be motivated for number 3.

Your mind will have a significant interest in number 4.

The other values are important to your mind, but they are not uppermost in terms of your mind's focus and drive.

The top 4 values are where your mind places emphasis. Are your top 4 values in keeping with your goals?

If not, you can add more focus on the (aspirational) values and order you would actually want using the following easy technique. Note: we don't change the number 1 value, that's very much a part of you and your personality, but elevating or adding a value into the number 2 or 3 position is a great way to give them a substantial boost.

ADDING FOCUS TO CHANGE YOUR VALUES

(a) Make a note of the one or two values you would like given a higher priority.

(b) Now actively notice where you already have that value. For example, let's say the value you would like to instal is 'freedom'. Think: where do I already have freedom? You can do this for even the most subtle 'freedoms'. E.g., freedom of what to wear, freedom of what to eat, freedom of what to drink, freedom of what to read. List as many examples as you can.

(c)   Continue to list as many examples as you can each day, for up to 30 days!

3. YOUR PREFERENCES

A third filter of the unconscious mind is that of preferences (also called metaprograms). Knowing your preferences and those of others is empowering and helps us to understand ourselves and others at a much deeper level and be more tolerant and flexible in our thinking about others.

To discover your preferences, think about the following questions. This table can also be found as a PDF at https://www.traceycolenlp.com/**riders-unlock-your-riding-success**/

Preferences	Note
1. Introvert/extrovert Are you an Introvert (someone who enjoys relaxing on their own) or an Extrovert (someone who enjoys relaxing with several others)? **"When it's time to recharge your batteries do you like to be alone or with someone else?" (How many people?).** **An introvert will appreciate quiet time alone to re-charge. An extrovert will need to be with others to fully re-charge.**	An introvert will need plenty of time on their own to relax and rejuvenate. An extrovert will need time with friends and / or family to relax and rejuvenate.
2. Details/big-picture Do you like descriptions with lots of details or do you like the big picture? **"Thinking about a riding skill, do you enjoy learning the nitty gritty or do you prefer to see the big picture of what you want to achieve?"**	A big-picture person may become bored by details. Give them the overview as well as necessary details. A details person may feel overwhelmed by the big picture. Give them mainly details.
3. Thinker/feeler Are you a logical thinker or do you get a feeling about things? Thinking – this person evaluates their world based on what they think about it – logic and reasonableness Feeling – more into values and feelings **"If you had a little problem to work through in your riding, would you use your logic to work out a solution or would you have a feeling about what to do?"**	Talk to the thinker in terms of logic and the feeler in terms of emotions. Note: a thinker may be able to handle stress to a greater extent. Never pressure a feeler, they may not be able to cope with added demands.
4. Spontaneous/planner Do you prefer to be more spontaneous or like to make and follow plans and routines? **"If you are going to go somewhere to do something do you want to plan it or do you want to just take it as it comes?"**	A spontaneous person will hate rigidity in training and will need some diversions. A planner will love routine and little change on the spur of the moment

5. Moving towards/away from in getting a goal
 	
"What do you want in a new horse?"
 	
If you mainly talk about what you _want_, you're more a towards person. If you talk about what you don't want, you're an away from person. More on this filter later – it underpins our focus and drive.
 	
    • Toward
    • <u>Toward with a little Away From</u>
    • Both Toward and Away From equally
    • Away From with a little Toward
    • Away From
	Towards people – remind them of their goal.
	
	Towards with a little away from – Here's the goal, here's a little of what we want to avoid.
	
	Both - Here's the goal, here's what we want to avoid.
	
	Away from with a little towards – We need to avoid these things, whilst working towards our goal
	
	Away from – let's avoid these mistakes

6. What motivates you?
 	
Why do you ride?
 	
    • <u>Possibility</u> (I can/could)
    • Necessity (I must/should/have to/need to)
    • Bit of both
	Possibility – talk to the rider using possibility words such as can, could, <u>is possible.</u>
	
	Necessity – talk to the rider in terms of necessity words such as must, need to, have to

7. Where does your feedback come from?
 	
How do you know when you're doing a good job?
 	
    • I know myself
    • I know when someone else tells me
    • Balanced
    • I know myself, but I like to have someone else say it too
    • I prefer others to tell me and I check in with myself to see if I agree
	The person who knows themselves cannot be convinced easily by others and vice versa.
	
	If a rider needs some external praise, remember to give it!
	
	If a rider needs some internal praise, tell them to tell themselves they did well.

8. How are you convinced? **How often do you have to do something well (e.g., jump a certain jump or ride a trot to canter transition) before you're convinced it's good?** <ul><li>If I do it once only</li><li>I have to do it a certain number of times (how many times?)</li><li>I have to do it over a certain time period (how long – how many hours, days or weeks?)</li><li>I'm never convinced!</li></ul>	This may impact the training, as the convincer filter is very powerful.
9. Taking action **When you have a challenge, do you usually act quickly after sizing it up, or do you do a complete study of all the consequences and then act?** <ul><li>Active – act right away</li><li>Reflective – think about it</li><li>Bit of both</li><li>Inactive – I don't act at all</li></ul>	This shows how much time, effort and energy someone will put into the work and the reflection. An active person needs to have a go right away, the reflective person times the time to consider.
10. Team/independent player **Tell me about a specific ride where you were the happiest.** <ul><li>Independent Player – you were riding/competing on your own</li><li>Team Player – you rode as part of a team</li><li>Management Player – you rode as part of a team and wanted to be captain or were the captain</li></ul>	Independent and team players need to train in such a way that meets their filtering, if possible. If a team player has to train on their own, it may be best to convince them that they are in partnership with their horse.
11. Response to stress **Tell me about a ride or a horse that gave you trouble, a one-time event.** <ul><li>Did you describe mostly what you were *thinking*?</li><li>Did you describe mostly what you were *feeling*?</li><li>Did it seem like you had a choice about whether to carry on or not?</li></ul> Mainly thinking – you handle stress well Mainly feeling – you handle low-level stress or none at all best If you felt like you had a choice, you may handle stress reasonably well	Knowing how a person copes in stressful situations enables us to know how much pressure they can take.

12. Your priorities: yourself and/or others
 	
If I were to ask you to write a couple of paragraphs about what you've been up to in the past few months, would you mainly write about
 	
     • Yourself? Is this because you find yourself less important/interesting or not?
     • Others? Is this because you find them more important/interesting or not?
     • Bit of both - balanced
	Knowing about this filter can make you aware of being too focussed on yourself or others.

13. How you process a challenge
 	
     • **When you need to work through a problem or a challenge in your life, is it absolutely necessary for you to:**
     • **Talk about it with someone else, or**
     • **Think about it by yourself on your own?**
         • External – with others
         • Internal – on your own
         • Both
	Another important filter for helping people when they have a challenge to sort out. What to do first: whether to leave them to think it through or to give them ideas and help.

14. Listening style
 	
     • **If someone you knew quite well and liked said to you, that they can't find any time to clean their tack/poo pick would you:**
     • **Find the comment interesting, but probably do nothing about it, or**
     • **Would you feel really compelled to help them?**
         • Literal – don't think about helping them
         • Inferential – pick up on hints
	If you have a literal listener, you'll have to speak to them directly and in literal terms. In you infer, they may not get what you want them to do.

15. Speaking style
 	
     • **If you felt that someone around you was not pulling their weight as well as they should, would you:**
     • **Tell them directly, or would you**
     • **Hint and give them clues and hope they get what you mean.**
         • Literal – very frank way of telling someone
         • Inferential – prefer to say things in a round about
	Imagine now, an inferential speaker listening to an inferential listener! Very little would be conveyed!

Knowing your preferences is a great way to play to your strengths. Knowing the preferences of someone you are coaching or supporting is a valuable means of giving them the type of support and feedback that may be crucial to their confidence and progress.

Complete the question set for the rider and the supporter. Are there any differences? It's always interesting to note how we all filter differently and to be aware that there are no rights or wrongs, simply different filtering.

Make a note of where you as a rider need to be supported more and you as a supporter can support more, in line with the rider's preferences.

2

THE POWER OF BEING
VULNERABLE - YOUR STRENGTHS
AND WEAKNESSES

BEING VULNERABLE

What does vulnerable mean to you? According to the dictionary being vulnerable means being exposed to the possibility of being attacked or harmed, either physically or mentally. Now we all know when we are riding there is an element of risk which means at some point we can be physically injured. I felt vulnerable after my injury (badly broken and dislocated ankle) because I wasn't able to do basic daily tasks until I regained strength and was allowed to weight bear. I couldn't move out of the way quickly enough if I needed to. I also was scared of slipping or falling on the ice which made me feel vulnerable. I had to ask for help, which seemed alien to me as I was so used to doing everything myself (see the values and beliefs chapter). How many times do you avoid asking for someone's help? Asking for someone's help is not being vulnerable, it should be empowering

27

because, with the best will in the world, we can't do everything ourselves. We shouldn't be overloading ourselves; we take better care of our mobile phones than we do ourselves in the equestrian world because if our phone is getting low on battery we charge it up.

However, what are your signs your batteries are getting low? Do you rush tasks? Are you short-tempered with people? Do you get frustrated easily?

If we think of the mental side for a moment. Grab a pen and paper for this exercise:

Imagine there is an invisible bubble around you.

- When do you feel vulnerable?
- Can you think of a moment in time when you felt this way? How did it feel and look to you? How did it sound?

Vulnerability can be waiting for a doctor to call you, being turned down, someone saying no, or not making a team selection.

Now, look at your emotions for each of your emotions. Go and reflect on how you are when you feel....... Sad, upset, fearful, angry, emotional?

- What does each of those emotions look and feel like to you?
- How do you act?
- What do you do?

- Why do they make you feel vulnerable?

Remember emotions are part of us, they are natural we all have them. The best readers of our emotions are our horses with their sixth sense. As humans, our senses are our hearing, sight, smell, taste and touch but horses also have a sixth sense, which means they can read your emotions, as they can match your heartbeat. This means that they know if you're happy, excited, scared, frightened and nervous.

We can't selectively numb our emotions by saying here's the good stuff and bad stuff, I only want to feel the good stuff. I don't want to feel disappointment, grief, fear, or shame. Instead, we try to perfect, which doesn't work as there is no such thing as perfection. Look up Brene Brown on YouTube and the power of vulnerability.

It's important that you know how you feel and react (triggers) when you are feeling each emotion so that you can press pause. By pressing pause you can give yourself a moment to collect yourself and gather your thoughts and emotions.

For example: If you are feeling nervous before your competition time. What things can you do to change that nervous feeling (feeling nervous is perfectly natural) to feeling confident or excited?

TIP

Many athletes use music as part of their warmup routines (practice in their training too) so that they can focus on what they are going to do and how they are going to react. Can you make yourself a playlist which makes you happy or excited? So, you can listen in the vehicle on your way to the competition and possibly when on your horse (depending on your horse – never have headphones in when riding on roads – as you need to be able to hear the other vehicles).

STAY HIDDEN OR BE SEEN?

Many people fear **becoming visible** because of fear of judgement and worthiness. The fear of what other people think of you and say about you. What is important to remember we are all humans, we can all make a mistake or get something wrong, and that's just how it is! As long as we own our own mistakes and learn from them that is what is important.

You need to be clear on whose opinion you value. The opinion that matters the most should be yours, so it is aligned with your values and beliefs. Does Joe Bloggs from another yard or someone from school's opinion matter to you? Have they acted out of jealousy or spite because you've done well, or do they think you've done better than them? What is that person feeling right now?

The key thing when reflecting on your experience, this could be comments on social media or what you've heard through gossip – is to think about the evidence. Did the person say what they meant to or have people changed the words as they've repeated their version (this is called distorting – which we all do. E.g., we all watch the same football match but we all will have a different version of events), experience and knowledge – does the person saying the thing have knowledge and experience (any qualifications, maybe competed at a certain affiliated level) themselves?

When things are typed – we can sometimes take them out of context because we haven't seen the person's body language and other communication indicators. The awareness of what other people are feeling in that moment (emotional intelligence), so our perception may differ.

"If we step into our power, then we will become seen. Being seen this will leave us open to people's opinions but remember your opinion matters the most, not anyone else's. **Vulnerability is the birthplace of belonging, joy, creativity, and love".**

I'm sure you can relate to the phrases below which makes us numb vulnerability:

"Stop crying, don't let them see, don't let them see you frightened or scared!"

Have you ever been told not to show your feelings if you are upset, scared, or frightened? So that your peers or other people don't see. Are you avoiding being vulnerable? Most of us have been conditioned to hide from being vulnerable but enough is enough. We need to stop giving others power over us. The power that they don't know they have. We need to make sure everyone knows that emotions are normal, they are natural, and we all need to be more supportive of others. By building a supportive community, we can all grow together, just like horses in their own heard.

STRENGTHS AND WEAKNESSES

Having things, we are good at and other areas we may have not mastered yet is normal. Many of us are either right or left-handed and some gifted people are ambidextrous (can use both hands), so we all have a stronger and weaker physical side.

If someone has a physical or mental disability doesn't mean that they have a weakness, it means they have a special gift which makes them unique. Putting labels on people sometimes limits our or their expectations of what they will be able to achieve. Where I look at it as, great we know what the disability is, now we can work out a plan to best support your needs and help you. As we can adapt our coaching methods, the space we are in, time frames, the equipment we use, and the place we are in can be adapted. We can also change the rules – nothing is set in stone as we adapt, evolve and progress. Many sports are examples of this. E.g., there is walking football and Boccia (para-sport similar to bowling, with precision ball placement).

Think about what are you wanting to achieve. What do you need to do? Do you need to make any adaptations? Remember STEP (Space, Time, Equipment and Place), so that you can be inclusive. As a rider write or talk through the answers to find out what would best help and support you. Remember nothing is fixed and be curious!

THREATS AND OPPORTUNITIES

Being aware of any potential threats to our riding or support network is important to know. Have a think of any threats which may affect your horse riding? E.g. not having your five freedoms (see chapter back yourself for Maslow's Hierarchy of Needs) includes money, safety, injuries, fear, others including competitors and peers. You can look and think of how you can make these into your strengths and find solutions to help improve these like increased fitness and self-care etc.

Then most importantly look for the opportunities around you. What opportunities can you find or see? Are there others wanting to work together on the same goal e.g. fitness, so you can hold each other accountable. Or where can you find or gain further knowledge? These opportunities don't always have to cost money. For example, going to competitions to watch, continuous professional development opportunities from governing bodies, cross country course walks, show jumping demonstrations, masterclasses, other riders, qualified coaches, talks, podcasts, other professionals from your farriers to physios, YouTube (carefully sifting through videos), horse and country tv etc.

SOCIAL MEDIA

Social Media has its advantages and is speeding up learning within the equestrian world, equestrian influencers can make an income from it, you can be in front of bigger audiences so that you can work with more people, connect with more people but it also has its disadvantages three main ones are:

1. Trolls.
2. People making dangerous silly content trying to chase viral likes and shares.
3. Bullies can follow children home now (so there is no rest away).

It is disgraceful when a fellow of the British Horse Society is often worried or threatened on social media by trolls. We need as an equestrian community to be better – better at communicating our views and better at filtering our views or videos or all comments we make. Rather than this culture of, "I'm right and they're wrong". People make that last statement as a certainty because the more afraid and vulnerable we are, the more afraid we are.

Be mindful that blame is often a way to discharge pain and discomfort. We need to be kind and open to listening to other people's opinions, views, values and beliefs. To have mutual respect so that we can create a safe space to share our knowledge and experiences. By improving education, we should be the change for our horses, which they deserve.

There is always another way of doing things, but we must make sure:

a)   Both Safety and welfare come first for both horses and riders.

b)   It is logical and able to understand the point of view.

c)   Evidence-based with scientific or research.

CHOICE

It's your choice, so you can choose how you show up, how you react, how you can choose to take your emotions or feelings out of the decisions you make, you can choose whom to listen to and whose opinions you value remembering you should value your own opinion first.

Opinions from someone else -are they qualified, have they got qualifications, what level of experience if they got, what knowledge have they got or skills? This could be other coaches, other riders, parents, peers or other loved ones.

We need to manage expectations by having clear boundaries and defined roles (what you expect from each other).

Parents or siblings or the person watching you (or even the person whom you would love to be watching you but aren't able to watch you) - what do they do which irritates you?

When do you start feeling nervous?

- When making entries for a competition.

- Travelling to the venue.
- Getting the horse ready.
- Warming up.
- During competition.
- Just after coming out of the arena.
- On your way home.

TIME FOR REFRAMING

Change your thoughts or opinions when something hasn't gone to plan. It's not a failure or disaster. This is your greatest lesson. These events are designed for you to grow and learn. these are your power (your fuel) to enable you to change and grow. So, stop sharing failures or classifying them as failures. They're not a bad thing or something to make fun of. These are so valuable for you to work out, what you need to do differently and how we can improve and develop your skills /knowledge to improve your performance. **At this moment, you get to choose how you react and where you're reacting from.**

EMPOWERMENT OF THE RIDER

You the rider need more ownership of what you're doing. So, if your coach says, 'good' ask them, 'What was good? Why was it good?' So that you both can get clearer on the detail and you can improve, but most importantly take and have owner-ship of what you have achieved.

TIPS FOR FEEDBACK

At the end of a session or even after you've ridden at a competition ask the following:

First, reflect on two *Stars* - things that went well or felt good (These are Positive reflections) and one *Wish* – the one thing you want to work on which will improve your performance (Here are some to get you started: Accuracy, Balance, Rhythm, Position, Timing etc).

Supporters - Parents or other loved ones.

Get a clicker counter to register every time you want to do the thing that irritates the rider, such as shouting, crossing your arms, giving them a funny look, then clap your hands and breathe out deeply (like a sigh – as if saying, *'For goodness sake, not again!'*).

How many times have you tried to do that during the session? Then repeat at the next session and see how few times you can do those things that irritate the rider.

Before you give your opinion to the rider, stop and think before you speak because it's not just your words that have power. It's your body language, the way you present yourself, the way you stand, where you stand, and your arms crossed (because you're cold but your rider thinks you're grumpy or annoyed).

I never want to hear a parent say to their child, *"That was rubbish"*, *"You fell off, you're meant to stay on"*, or *"That was a demolition round"*.

TOP TIP

Instead, you need to get the rider to tell you in their own words how it felt to them. Ask them for *Two Stars and a Wish*. So that you can get them to start in a positive frame of mind. There will always be positives to take away home. Here are some hints - control, rhythm, balance, lines, accuracy, position, control of the lower leg, weight on their stirrups, upper body, hands, feel, timing and different paces (walk, trot, canter). Ask them, *'how did it feel to you?'* we need to not put our thoughts onto them, as they have to be able to make decisions for themselves and be given the opportunity to take ownership of what they are doing to enable them to develop their skills and knowledge, enabling them to learn and grow.

Two key words to **make sure you are all clear on** our **Perception** and **Ownership.** Keep checking to make sure you are on **the same page.**

Responsibility is for everyone involved with a rider to make sure they are behaving appropriately with the self-control of their own emotions. You'll learn more about managing expectations in the chapter on building successful relationships.

HERE'S A GREAT EXERCISE FOR PROMOTING OR STARTING CONVERSATIONS:

Example 1: Your supporter (mum, dad, sibling, loved one or friend), is standing away in the corner, watching you from a distance compete, with her arms crossed and looks like she has her mad face on.

- How would this make you feel?
- What does look like to you?
- How would you react?
- Can you remember when you last felt (insert emotion), what happened?
- Pause – take time to process and respond (Don't let anyone finish your sentences for you).

Now time to write two actions.

- How can you react differently? Find out why it annoys you and be honest.
- How can you get, the person to do a different action? Can you give them a clicker e.g., for every time they try to shout something at you over the fence? So, they can realise how many times they do the said behaviour.

Example 2: You might be in the warm-up ring and you hear another competitor saying they "don't like the look of fence 7". You may have already been feeling nervous about fence 7 or you may have been thinking you're looking forward to jumping all the fences because it looks straightforward (balance, rhythm, straight lines and use your corners).

- How would this make you feel?
- What does look like to you?
- How would you react?
- Can you remember when you last felt (insert emotion), what happened?

- Pause – take time to process and respond (Don't let anyone finish your sentences for you).
- Now time to write two actions.
- How can you react differently? Find out why it annoys you and be honest.
- What can you do, to not let other people's opinions bother you? Not to listen, take it with a pinch of salt, go and visualise your own round. Make sure you have your own performance clear on what you are going to do.

Write this down, so you can start mapping out your own plan.

3

UNDERSTAND YOUR STORY: WHAT UNDERPINS YOUR FOCUS AND DRIVE?

Focus enables an equestrian to respond to the cues from the horse and the job at hand. It's a means of concentrating on what's important and controllable and de-focusing on the rest. Drive is one of those internal factors and is why we do what we do. What's the aim, is it the joy of riding or competing or something else? Understanding where our focus and drive come from is important in maintaining or elevating them. (See later chapter for more on how to increase motivation.)

What marks out an expert in their field is the ability to remain calm and continue to place their attention on only the cues that are performance-related. In addition, champions can sustain their drive by knowing what motivates them and reminding themselves of the goal and how far they have come rather than each individual ride.

The good news is that both focus and drive can, to a large extent, be enhanced. As a starting point, let's delve into your own focus and drive to find out more about YOU!

FOCUS

Focus can be external or internal. For example, are you more inside your own world, your own head? Are you more focused on the outside environment? As a rider, it's good to have a certain flexibility of focus. However, developing a more internal focus is the aim. If your focus is entirely on what your horse is doing, where their head is, and how they will react to a spooky corner or something else around you, then you'll not ride in a responsive way, you'll be waiting for the horse to (re)act first.

Riding with your 'floorplan' in your head, knowing where you are in the arena or on a hack and what you want to do from moment to moment as if you're choreographing the steps, is a superb style of focus. However, if you're entirely within your own head, you may not notice something important. Riders ideally have a very much internal focus, with a very slight external focus.

Focus can also be described as broad or narrow; once again there is a sweet spot for your concentration. If the focus is too narrow, you may only be concentrating on one small aspect of your riding, e.g., the position of your hands or whether your heels are in the correct place. This may cause other misalignments or problems.

If your focus is too broad, e.g., you are thinking about everything in your environment, from people walking by the arena to various noises, dogs, horses etc. You aren't thinking about the ride and yourself as a rider.

Flexibility in your focus is key again. Being able to call back your focus to your ride and what you're doing, rather than focusing on the outside, whilst being able to assess your riding and your horse's way of going is something worthy of practice.

The following table can also be found as a PDF at:

https://www.traceycolenlp.com/**riders-unlock-your-riding-success**/

	Narrow	Broad
Internal	Good for getting into the zone, perfecting a specific skill e.g., where to carry your hands.	Good for evaluating your performance, the rider overall.
External	Good for assessing the horse and a specific aspect of their movement e.g., whether they are using their hind end well.	Good on hack when quickly assessing the environment.

CONSIDER THE FOLLOWING QUESTIONS

1. Where is your attention at any time during your ride?
2. Where is your attention when you lead your horse or warm your horse up?

3. Where is your attention when doing flatwork, dressage, show-jumping, cross-country jumping, hacking or other types of riding?
4. Where is your attention when you have a lesson? How is that different from riding on your own?
5. Where is your attention if someone is watching you?
6. Think about the different types of riding you do. Make a list, e.g., flat work, jumping, ground work etc. Then decide where the optimal attention for a rider would be. Start to work towards this, very gradually, taking one type of riding at a time, until you have mastered your attention. We'll be looking at techniques to support you in your focus later.
7. If you are a supporter of a rider, where is your attention when they ride? Consider, whether is it narrow or broad. Do you think you have the balance right?

Now rate your focus for 1-7 above – is it a healthy focus?

INTERNAL AND EXTERNAL MOTIVATION

CARROT AND STICK?

Are you a carrot or a stick person? Do you prefer to be held to account or is a more supportive approach better for your progression? If you had a piece of work to be handed in on a specific date, would the fear of the deadline and burning the midnight oil to meet it be more your style? Or, would you rather get it finished so that you weren't under so much pressure?

Do you need a 'threat' of the stick to get you motivated and to stay motivated? Do you prefer the more positive-reinforcement approach of the carrot?

The carrot people are called 'towards' and the stick people, are 'away from'. You can be anywhere in between these two categories too. For example, you could be mainly a towards person, with a little away.

What people don't realise is that carrot and stick people have the same goal. However, the towards person is all about focusing on the goal and the stick person focuses on the negatives; they aim to get to the goal by moving away from the unpleasantness. For example, if you have a project to complete, do you get it done so that you can enjoy the satisfaction of having completed it or do wait for the threat of a deadline? A towards-person is focusing on the pleasantness of doing the project; the away-from person wants to get the project done but in a far less agreeable manner.

If you investigated your preferences (metaprograms) previously, you may already have some idea of how your filter works.

To find out which style of filter is most natural for you, think about 5-10 things to look for when buying a new horse or pony.

1.	6.
2.	7.
3.	8.
4.	9.
5.	10.

Now, did you list mostly qualities you want or mostly qualities you don't want? If you said mostly the qualities you want, then you are a towards person, whereas if you mostly listed qualities that you don't want, then you're an away from person.

You can, of course, be partly towards and partly away from. This type of person will move somewhat towards a goal, yet may be held back by fears or discomfort.

Let's take the example of two equestrians wanting to achieve success in competition.

They both have the same goal, compete in the same competitions and have the same level of skill, experience and physical ability. I'm going to call them after my mares, Lottie and Darci.

Lottie looks forward to her competition day, she's trained hard and wants to do well. She's ready! She learns from past errors and works hard to go beyond them. She wants to improve on her results from last time and she's often thinking and visualising exactly how she wants the competition to go.

- Area of main **Focus: doing well.** Moving towards her goals by focusing on positive outcomes.
- Mindset attitude: positive reinforcement and reward.

- Direction filter: towards.

Darci wants to do well too, just as well as Lottie, she's trained hard too and she wants to continue to improve. She's also worked hard on correcting errors. But she's concentrating on her mistakes from the last few competitions, she focuses on what went wrong, what could go wrong and how awful she'll feel if she makes those same mistakes again. Or, more mistakes.

- Area of main **Focus: not messing up.** Moving towards her goals by running away from negative outcomes.
- Mindset attitude: fear-based punishment and anguish.
- Direction filter: away from

Most elite riders have mostly towards thinking and a little away from (the away from is good for recognising errors and risks and adjusting to overcome them).

Having too little towards means that the rider is fear-driven and the ride isn't very enjoyable. Too little away from and the rider may not learn from mistakes or may not account for the usual potential risks associated with riding.

Away from people may yo-yo from relative success to relatively unsuccessful times, this is because once an away from person reaches their goals, they no longer have the stick in place to motivate them. They begin to self-sabotage to unconsciously bring back a stick!

Away from preferences are fear-based; with fear being such a potent emotion, it requires lots of energy to maintain an away from set of values, beliefs and goals.

Having said that, there are certain advantages to being away from: you will spot errors and risks easily. It's how you then manage your criticism and lack of risk-taking so that you can ride the way you want to.

In being coached, if an away from person is finding it too challenging to achieve goals and sustain them, NLP and other psychological techniques can help to easily move them towards being a towards person! To do this, fear is usually removed, together with the inner conflicts that can be present in an away from mentality.

Notice where you may be more towards and away from. Notice whether you feel you might want to change your perspective or whether your preferences work perfectly for you.

4

BACK YOURSELF (SELF-BELIEF)

I magine you're in a race, with your own experience and skills. With the decisions you've already made, now imagine there's only you in the race. You have to back yourself to win. You're in your own lane, focusing on your journey. There is not always a direct route to getting where you want to go but if you have a plan which is written down, put in the hard work and believe you will get there because you will. This is like me becoming a UKCC level 4 Coach, working from the bottom up. Everyone starts somewhere but it's so important that everyone's journeys are completely different, gaining valuable knowledge, skills, timing, reactions, and decisions.

You need to believe in yourself, that you are good enough to do what you want to. You are more than capable of achieving your goals, targets and dreams. You are the most important person in your riding/coaching career. Don't let anyone pull

CLAIRE NIXON-ORD UKCC LEVEL 4 COACH & TRACEY COLE BSC, PHD

you apart and most importantly back yourself. Start believing in yourself.

You may need to gain more experience, different skills and knowledge and develop weaknesses but that is all possible!

MOTIVATION

One of the key parts of self-belief is motivation. What drives you to achieve your goals, targets and dreams? It is important to find out what drives you.

Is it an internal motivation or an external motivation (need a qualification for a job or to make someone else happy)?

Maslow's Hierarchy of Needs describes how a person's five freedoms must be met (food, water, shelter, freedom to be a person and free from injury and disease) and their psychological needs, for them to feel safe. This enables them to be motivated to gain up to their self-fulfilment needs in achieving their potential.

Whereas the Dent and Reynolds Theory says you must build the relationship, create the environment and then you can steepen the learning curve.

Also, to factor in is the number of times people are achieving rather than failing (they need to be achieving 70%).

Grab a pen and write your answers to the following questions:

1. When do you feel most motivated to be at your best?
2. When do you feel least motivated to be at your best?
3. What patterns of your behaviour do you notice when it comes to motivating yourself to achieve your goals?
4. Are there any rules you must follow to motivate yourself?
5. Is there anything you do to motivate yourself? E.g., a reward once you've achieved the goal?

Thinking of the 4 areas of motivation - autonomy (things happen automatically), Belonging (our sense of feeling we belong there in e.g. a herd, group, environment or competition), Competence or mastery (mastering a subject, performing the thing without thinking about it) and Meaning (why you are doing something). We need to explore deeper so that we can understand your motivations.

AUTONOMY

1. When do you feel in control of your actions and decisions?
2. When are you free to make your own choices?
3. Can you remember a time when you were in control? How did it make you feel?
4. How does it feel when it doesn't go to plan? What are the lessons you take away from the experience?

BELONGING

1. How do you feel in new environments?
2. Do you find it easy to make new friends?
3. If you're at a party do you go over and start a conversation?
4. Where did you last feel part of a community? How did that feel?

COMPETENCE / MASTERY

1. How do you know if you've mastered something?
2. What makes you feel effective in the actions you make and the decisions you've made?
3. What stands out to you?

MEANING

1. When do you know "Why" you are doing something?
2. Is your Why for you or do you like pleasing others?

By getting clear on how you work in situations or in the moment, this really helps you to understand how you can change, how you are showing up because you are identifying the triggers or things which cause you to react. You can identify the way you want to respond or react in events or occurrences, to what you currently do. With this knowledge you can then action the steps which you need to take to change your learnt behaviours. E.g. instead of feeling nervous, what can you do to make you feel excited? How can you change the environment you're in e.g. music your listening to, warm up routines (wearing your competition gear at home, so that it doesn't feel any different to when you're at home), being organised to keep you calm and relaxed etc.

PART II

RIDER

In this section, you will get clear on what you want to achieve and how you're going to achieve it!

5

GETTING IN FOCUS

The level of focus in a rider can be learnt. For some riders who compete, there may be a long day of different classes and a need to be able to focus and re-focus at will. Luckily, focus and having the flexibility to re-focus after a break, can be learnt. Training mentally in this way is equally as important as training physically and can be the edge that a competitor needs to make a difference.

In the previous section, we discussed how focus can be external, internal, narrow or broad. As a rider, it's important that you have the flexibility to use these types of attention to get the best from the task you're performing. For example, in schooling your horse to do a new movement, your attention may be on the horse and the feel of the horse (external), with some narrow focus on precision. If you were at a competition performing that movement in a dressage test, your focus may be on recalling the test (internal), the feel of the horse and your aids (external) and may be narrow to exclude outside distractions, yet broad enough to have the peripheral vision to be able to see a good portion of the arena.

Notice that in the example above, distractions are not a point of focus. Whether the distraction is external (the weather, other riders, other people watching, lorries and cars passing by the arena etc.) or internal (reviewing past experiences, comparing yourself to another rider and 'what-ifs'). Having an incorrect focus can rapidly change how someone rides. For example, most riders have experienced freezing during a ride, lesson, competition or clinic. This is when they seem physically unable to move effectively, give aid or ride well. It's a time when the attentional focus is shining on you as the rider and all the fears you might have. It's the ultimate internal focus on all the negatives that makes us 'choke' as athletes.

In this section, we'll look more closely at removing different types of distractions, as well as improving concentration and re-focusing after the focus has been broken.

1. INTERNAL DISTRACTIONS

Our minds are often overly busy and what's going on inside our heads can be a huge distraction. Whether we're contemplating our fears, past events, what-ifs or negative self-talk, internal distractions form a barrier to achieving the right focus.

ANXIETY

Fears and anxiety are seldom real. Anxieties come from focusing on the future, not the present. In the moment, if our horse spooks or reacts badly in some way, we can generally cope. We enter into an automatic mode of action. There's little time to think, we simply act. Anxiety has not helped us. It may even have hindered us, because transmitting those nerves to your horse may make them anxious and on high alert too.

Here's another way to think about anxiety: it's a signal that you're not focusing on what you want to happen, you're focusing on what you don't want to happen!

Remember in that case, that by focusing on what we want, we dimmish the anxiety. Bring your focus away from what you don't want and only focus on what you do want – this is very important!

There are several quick and easy neurolinguistic programming (NLP) techniques to dissolve anxiety and nerves. Here are two examples.

a. Changing how your mind is programmed to think about the anxious feeling

1. Consider what makes you anxious and as you think about that, where does the anxious feeling start in your body?
2. Where does that anxious feeling go to?

3. Can you will the feeling to go somewhere else, e.g., your big toe? If the feeling won't budge, no matter.

4. What colour is that feeling? Now, will the colour change to your favourite colour or some other colour that will enable the anxiety to dispel

5. Is the feeling spinning? Clockwise or ant-clockwise? Can you will the feeling's spin to change direction?

Notes

a.   Any change of the feeling in terms of its location, pathway, colour or 'spin' will lessen anxiety.

b.   There are no rules with this technique, you can change the anxiety feeling to anything other than how you currently do it

c.   Work on this technique frequently so that you can rid yourself of the anxiety more quickly each time.

b. Changing how you think about an event that you have planned, but it's making you nervous.

1. Imagine you're 15 minutes after the successful completion of the event. You have to imagine 100% success; if you have doubts or worries, this process won't work 100%. So, make sure what you see/hear/feel about that future event is utterly compelling and successful. Imagine 15 minutes after that completely successful outcome.

2. Now ask yourself, where's the anxiety?

3. If it's gone, repeat this exercise when the slightest nerves just begin to return.

4. If you still feel anxiety, it's simply because you haven't yet imagined 100% success. You may have imagined 90 or 95%! Remember, this is only in your imagination, not reality. You can imagine anything! You can imagine that you're an Olympian or that you're riding a talking horse(!), so now just imagine that event as being successful.

5. Repeat step 4 until the anxiety has gone – as soon as you imagine that the event is a total success, the anxiety will leave.

PAST EVENTS

If there is something in the past that affects how you think and ride, maybe an old accident, trauma or fall, it's best to consult a practitioner of Time Line Therapy® who has an equestrian specialism. They can help you to remove the emotional charge of the old event and prevent it from springing into your mind as you ride.

NEGATIVE THOUGHTS AND WHAT IFS

Intrusive thoughts can pop into your mind uninvited and can bring with them the negative what-if disaster movies. There are different ways of stopping these things putting in an appearance. These come under the term 'pattern interrupt'. The pattern is another word for a habit because feeling nervous can be thought of as a habit. Thoughts, words, images and mini-movies running through our heads only do so because we haven't pressed a stop switch.

The mind will continue to send us these negatives until we override them. Doing that is easy, but getting the mind into the new habit requires practice until that too happens automatically.

There are different means of stopping the old pattern, try them on and see which one works for you.

a.   Saying a word that makes your mind sit up and listen! This could be a loud and very firm STOP! Or ENOUGH! Say the word at the first sign of nerves and continue to say it until you've battered the nerves down. You can say it out loud or inside your head.
b.   Sing! Singing does quite a bit for nervousness. It helps us to breathe a little more deeply, it causes us to think about something else – i.e., we have to remember the words and tune and it uplifts our spirits.
c.   If your thoughts come to you as words you can hear, change the voice into a silly voice such as that of Donald Duck. Aim to turn the sound down too.

If you get in with a pattern interrupt early enough, which means when you first start with the nerves, and you do your pattern interrupt often enough, your pattern will change. Repeat this as often as needed until you no longer run the old pattern.

2. EXTERNAL DISTRACTION

If you're distracted by people, horses and other things going on around you when you ride, there are ways to diminish these diversions in your focus.

PEOPLE WATCHING YOU

This is a common outside distraction. We assume that 1. people are watching us and 2. they are being judgemental in an unkind way. Have you ever stood by the side of an arena and not been very aware of the round taking place? Have you ever watched a round and willed the rider to do well?

In all likelihood, the spectators are probably not watching you closely nor analysing your performance. However, here's a technique that can help you to maintain a good focus on your riding, without needing to think about other people.

This technique uses peripheral vision. When we enter into full peripheral vision, we block out negative thoughts and feelings. Practise getting into peripheral vision whilst unmounted at first. Then try it in walk, for example for half of the school, building up to a whole circuit of the school. Finally, build up to riding like this for the majority of the time.

1. Pick a spot above your eye line in front of you. Keep focusing on that spot, taking in all the colours, textures, light/shadow and focussing in.
2. Keep going for about 20 seconds.

CLAIRE NIXON-ORD UKCC LEVEL 4 COACH & TRACEY COLE BSC, PHD

3. Now allow your vision to extend slightly, so that you are looking at the spot and about 30cm on either side, slowly take your vision out a little more and more until you can't focus on the spot, but you can see your hands if you stretch your arms out level with your shoulders.

4. Now stretch your vision even wider. Now you're in peripheral vision. Look directly in front, down or around and maintain a wide vision.

5. If you start to think about people watching you ride, you will probably drop out of peripheral vision, as you focus on the negative thoughts and feelings.

6. Bring your vision back to peripheral vision. You'll start to relax a little more and push those negative thoughts away.

NOISES

Noises around your yard or when you're out riding some-where, whether traffic, construction work or even the calling of another horse, are quite off-putting! However, the more you pay attention to the noise, the more you alert your horse. Even if your horse becomes aware and distracted before you do, your attention on the noise exacerbates the horse's lack of attention.

The first thing to do is to stop yourself from listening to or listening out for noise. Use the peripheral vision exercise from above, this will enable you to be calm, yet aware of noises. In addition, block the noise by humming or talking to yourself. You can turn your ride into a mindful ride. By this, we mean start to give yourself a running set of instructions. For example, if you were in a school, you could say, "Walk a 20m circle at A," as you walk around the circle, consider the horse's way of going and comment on it, tell yourself to apply more inside leg or more outside hand and continue to manoeuvre around the school with this constant style of instructions and comments on what's happening.

YOUR HORSE IS BEING ANXIOUS, NAPPY OR SPOOKY.

Again, riders know that the horse mirrors the rider's level of anxiety and nerves. To keep the horse going forwards and moving his/her feet, in lots of different shapes around the school (or if on a hack, add in changes of pace within a gait, leg yield, shoulder in etc.), use the commentary method describe in the paragraph above. Keep in peripheral vision too, to maintain your calmness.

You can also put in lots of circles – e.g., if your horse is spooky about something at the end of the school, pop in a 10 m circle. Keep their focus towards the inside of the school by giving your inside rein a little tickle and release as soon as the horse is looking inwards. Then continue on your route. If your horse becomes spooky again, add a little circle and relax – your job here is not one of perfection in schooling, but in getting your horse's focus back. You may not get out of walk! But you will get the focus and can continue your schooling on another day.

Remember that abandoning a schooling plan is not a failure, but a valuable lesson to you and your horse. You know how to regain your horse's focus instead of pushing through a messy schooling session. Your horse knows they can relax, all is well.

ANTICIPATE DISTRACTIONS.

Practising your ride with controlled distractions can be quite good fun! You can do this on the ground and then mounted when you have the confidence to do so. Have a supporter place a tablecloth over the fencing around the school or over a jump wing, even better if there is a breeze! Ask someone to drive past you in their car, turn on a hose or open an umbrella (slowly at first with this one!), place pots of flowers around the school etc.

By giving you and your horse these very controlled situations, where the distraction is built up gradually and where there may only be one distraction per schooling session.

3. WHAT OTHERS SAY OR DO – COMPARING YOURSELF

Healthy and balanced comparisons can act as a form of goal setting. However, riders tend not to do this! There can be a kind of comparison that's tinged with envy and that's certainly not healthy. Young riders need to steer clear of this type of comparison – not least because young bodies develop at different rates, so even a comparison with a peer may not be suitable, as that person could be physically stronger, not going through growth spurts or the huge impact of hormonal changes.

Comparison of the maladaptive (unhealthy) type is a form of perfectionism. It's an upward comparison that can lead to feelings of inferiority and the creation of self-limiting beliefs, such as, "I'm not good enough." If not kept in check, the focus is more on the other rider than on yourself. This loss of focus could lead to a loss of concentration and loss of performance.

Bringing your attention back to your progression is bringing yourself back into balance. Rather than accentuating others' good points, aim to work on your own weaker points. It's a shift of perspective that pays dividends and is the basis of becoming a more resilient athlete; focused on yourself, your riding and your improvement.

It can be a very empowering exercise to make a list of your accomplishments, big and small, even minute victories count! It doesn't have to be winning, it could be overcoming a hurdle or teaching yourself to stay calm or schooling your horse through a new movement. You could have a notebook specifically for this type of mindset work. Add to this list every week. Use the list to look back and acknowledge how far you have come. This notebook can also contain your goal setting (see later for tips on how to do this).

Lastly, avoid being triggered. Know what your trigger points are and delete them (see later). A more realistic perception of yourself as a rider can also help and that's what we're discussing later on.

CLAIRE NIXON-ORD UKCC LEVEL 4 COACH & TRACEY COLE BSC, PHD

REFOCUSING

As riders, there are times when we need full-on focus and that could be followed by downtime, such as a break between classes or a time when we're not riding in a shared lesson clinic.

How then, can you bring your focus back after a break?

Here's a handy technique to enable you to get into the zone quickly!

1. Think of a word or phrase that you'd like to use as a signal to refocus. It could be 'focus' or 'it's time' or 'let's do it'.
2. Now think of being in laser-sharp focus when riding, think about how that emotion of full focus feels, really feel it very strongly in your body. When you have that focus feeling as strong and intense as you can make it, say your refocus phrase.
3. When you want to be focused again, repeat this word to yourself. If you want the focus to come back even more, repeat steps 1-3.

FLOW STATE

Flow state in sports means being totally in the zone, where nothing can phase you and no intrusive thoughts or the external environment can disrupt your performance. You know that when it matters, you are putting into practice the hours of training and learning; this is not a time to be distracted by goals, but a time to simply set aside everything other than riding in the moment.

The flow state is where your peak performance happens. It's not an easy state to be in, yet it differentiates the elite athletes from everyone else.

One way to begin to get into your flow state is to practise the peripheral vision exercise often, use it when you are at home, in a car, doing chores, watching television, or sweeping the yard – practise until you can enter that state of calm confidence and determination.

6

GOAL SETTING

Traditionally we've been brought up with the concept of thinking of a goal you want to achieve by a certain date and working backwards from that date to determine how you are going to achieve that goal. This is sometimes like selecting the goal and throwing it up onto the wall, sometimes hit and miss whether you achieve the goal.

For you to be successful in achieving your goal it is vital to get clear on what you want to achieve and your *why* (internal driving force otherwise known as your motivation).

Exercise: I want you to write down your answers to the following questions:

1. Decide what goal you want to achieve.
2. Why do you want to achieve this goal?
3. Where are you now?

4. What will you see, hear, feel, taste, and smell, when you have it?
5. What does it mean for you to achieve this goal?
6. How will it feel for you to achieve this goal?
7. How will you know you have it?
8. What will this goal get you or allow you to do?
9. What do you have now, and what do you need to achieve your goal?

Goals are often described as long-term, medium goal, and short-term goals. I want you to take your long-term goal with a realistic date of achievement and write it down.

We also need to assess your current starting point of where you are now with your experience, skills and knowledge you have already. Profile wheels are great at getting you to evaluate your performance. If you haven't already done so, please visit Chapter 2 (Power of being vulnerable – including Your strengths and weaknesses) so you can be clear on your strengths and weaknesses, with areas for development.

Now for you to achieve this goal we must get clear on the process which is required for your goal. You need to know what you need to do, what skills you need to develop and knowledge and practice to enable you to achieve these goals.

I find qualifications an easier goal to break down because you have a clear list of criteria for you to achieve the assessment goal. Whereas if you compare British Dressage Pet Plan Area festivals qualifying for Badminton grassroots championships, they are a little harder to quantify what you need to do to achieve your qualifications – although you know you have to have 3 scores at 60% and above. Whereas in British Eventing to qualify, you have to finish in the top 10/20% (depending on the championship) of BE90 and BE100- which means you can become reliant on other competitors' results on the day to qualify.

If we take the ultimate goal of achieving your BHSI (Performance Coach Eventing) as an example of your long-term goal. Look at the assessment entry requirements (you will have to achieve your BHS Stages 1, BHS Ride Safe and 2,3,4 before you can enter the assessment in complete horsemanship – however there is now the option for Dressage and Show Jumping Specific from BHS Stage 3 upwards) and then the criteria of the assessment.

Then break it down into the three assessment areas Care and Welfare (management), Riding (training horses to lunge and ride) and Coaching (training and development of partnerships).

Now before the overwhelm sets in, we need to break this goal down into each section. The best thing to do is get a highlighter and highlight the keywords.

BHSI – TRAINING HORSES (LUNGING AND RIDING).

If we take the training horses section, we know that to achieve this assessment riders must be able to train horses both on the ground and ridden. They must assess horses' way of going, being clear with their own training philosophies, methods, and their experience of training horses for dressage up to advanced medium, eventing to BE Novice level (1.10m cross country) and Show Jumping to Foxhunter level (1.20m).

This is no mean task to ride horses you haven't ridden before, to ride them up to that level is a big ask because you must be able to develop a rapport and relationship with that horse within 30-45 minutes. You will need to be riding fit, if you have an injury or disability you can apply for a reasonable adjustment but must still be able to show you can ride to the level. I always advise riders who are wanting to progress through the levels, to work on achieving their riding first before they have injuries or lose their suppleness.

To make this even easier I've broken them down into six sections with the assessment times divided (3 hours 30 minutes):

1. 45 minutes- Assessing horse for purchase or on behalf of clients. Will need to be able to assess a horse statically, moving and ridden including the horses

2. 15 minutes- Riding and Training Theory – Training Logbook 6 months training programme with a horse you've been working with.

3. 1 hour- Riding – Dressage up to Advanced Medium (will need to know fitness level required, competition rules including what all is involved in Intro, Prelim, Novice, Elementary, Medium, Advanced Medium

and Advanced for future development of the horse to move up to the next level).

4. 30 minutes- Show Jumping – up to Foxhunter 1.20m (You will need to know competition rules, distances, speeds, fitness level required and the British Show Jumping competitions - first rounds British Novice 90cm, Discovery 1m, Newcomers 1.10m, Foxhunter 1.20m and then National Classes – important to know There are four categories within the British show jumping senior competitions, they are Club, Category 1, Category 2 and Category 3. For juniors there are Just for Schools, Club and Junior events).

5. 30 minutes - Cross Country – up to 1.10m (BE rules, distances, fitness requirements, types of fences, avoiding dehydration, muscle fatigue and competitions BE80, BE90, BE100, BE105, BE Novice and Intermediate).

6. 30 minutes- Lunging and Long reining - Training horses on the Ground with one rein and two. Training gadgets, methods of training including clicker training and new ways of thinking (Equitation science and research), training over poles, and clear understanding of what you are wanting to develop and achieve.

For each of the sections, it would be a good idea to work out your key areas (keywords- which are measurable) for development for you to make your training plan. You can make these into a word tree.

For example: In Section 3 - Training horses (Lunge and Ride)- The Dressage Section.

For each of the horses you ride, you can divide it into 4 sections:

1)   Warm up – Check equipment, horse description (age horse, sex of horse, height, breed, type, any conformational, shoes, any injuries – spot the obvious e.g., if the horse has a scar or is missing an eye all things riders can miss under pressure).

a)   What do you want to check in your warm-up – breaks, steering, reactions, listening, rhythm, stiffness, equal on both reins, connection into the contact (not on an outline but listening to the rider), your position, effectiveness, horse's temperament, stride length and general feel.

2)   Main Session – Finding out what your horse can do, what they struggle with or find easy. Giving them a mark (as if you were riding a test). What exercises can you do to improve and develop the horse's way of going? Are they stuck in a certain tempo or are they struggling with suppleness or straightness?

b)   Go through your scales of training and have at least 3 ways to help improve obedience, balance, rhythm, suppleness, Contact, Impulsion, Straightness and Collection. For each of the dressage, levels have knowledge of what exercise movements and paces come into each level of progression.

3)   Cool Down – slowing down the tempo, stretching, free walk on a long rein, starting to evaluate own and horses' performance in own head.

4) Summary – reflections on the horse compared to the scales of training, what you felt and did and marks you would have awarded before and afterwards. Areas for future development with the training plan of what you would do if you had this horse in your yard including fitness plan (hacking, gallops, water treadmills, alternative therapies, magnets, salt chambers etc), training, competitions you would be aiming to compete at etc. Include all the people you would need in your team (e.g. owners, vets, farriers, physios, saddlers, nutritionists, biomechanics analysis, coaches etc) to best help support you both.

Here's an example of a think tree:

PROFILE WHEEL

Once you've worked out exactly what you need to do, to achieve your goal. Then it is a good idea for you to identify 8 keywords in your own language pattern (of attributes you need to achieve your goal). These can be related to the performance of what you need to do to achieve your goal e.g., knowledge, skills, balance, reaction time, position, focus, mental clarity under pressure etc. Fill in the words and then colour to where you currently feel you are. If your coach can do the same would be great. Then you can compare the two, to see if you are being fair to yourself or sometimes being hard on yourself.

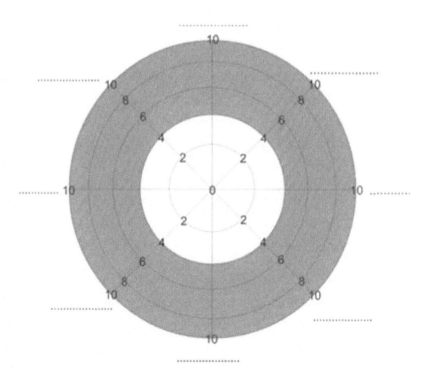

By completing a profile wheel you will then have a clearer idea of where you are and what areas you need to focus on to achieve your goal.

Every task we do has a process whether we are conscious about the process or are doing it unconsciously competent because it is second nature. The more experience, knowledge and skills that we gain improve our riding process (small things we do, to make the whole picture come together).

Our process is driven from within by what we decide on what success means to us and what it looks like to us. We set our goals to achieve our dreams and ambitions. Many people can have different ideas on what success means e.g., is it winning a competition gaining something tangible like a medal or rosette or taking part in a competition or gaining a qualification or having fun enjoying learning and participating in a sport you love?

We always can continually improve but we need self-awareness, CPD (continuous professional development), self-reflection and evaluation of our coaching.

With goals we must make them achievable, sometimes that's into smaller goals so that you can achieve the bigger goal. Celebrate the wins in between with something that makes you feel good e.g., this could be a little treat for yourself or a celebration with loved ones.

Take time to celebrate! You deserve to!

TOP TIPS: HOW TO STICK AT YOUR GOALS;

1. Write them down on post notes (each thing you need to do, each day to work towards that goal). Taking them down after you've done them. Maybe start with a 9-day challenge, then build up the days to 21, 35, 45, 55, 65, 75 etc). Until these positive changes become your routine.
2. Maybe have a photo of the goal that you're trying to achieve.
3. Affirmations – like *"I am a BHSI loving helping the partnerships I coach"* or *"I have competed at HOYS with my horse in 2024!"*.
4. Set up milestones, so that you can celebrate as you keep achieving your goals.

7

BUILDING SUCCESSFUL RELATIONSHIPS

For us to establish and build successful relationships we need to make sure that we are clear in our communication so that we can build a relationship with trust. Setting boundaries of what we both expect in black and white makes this so much easier. E.g., when you are available to be contacted on your phone or social media unless there is an emergency.

The use of performance conversations is great to get conversations started but more importantly so that we can be clear on what you want to achieve, how you are going to achieve it and how we can best support the rider.

IGNITE YOUR MOTIVATION.

Motivation is an emotion, it's built in a series of steps as shown in the diagram. First of all, the right environment for learning, one which is supportive and positive is needed for an easier pathway to being motivated. This promotes the emotions that are conducive to motivation: the enjoyment of learning and the enjoyment of success, no matter how small or large the success might be. Once these are in place, motivation is beginning to grow. There is a desire, a wanting to experience more or change so that success can follow.

This gives us the motivation to learn more and in doing so, gain self-confidence and self-belief to keep going and continue to learn. As we begin to hone our skills, focus and know our goals, our motivation increases, which spurs us more as we start the cycle again, this time with a higher level of knowledge, experience and skills.

In this section, we will take a look at what facets of motivation we can improve and how to do so. We'll look at the mental and emotional aspects, in particular, self-confidence, self-belief, and expectations and remove aspects that decrease our motivation. We've already talked about focus, goals and values, all of which also play a role in being sufficiently motivated.

YOUR SELF-BELIEF

It's important to take the time to evaluate your self-belief. Not necessarily what you tell others, but that deeper fundamental belief you have in your ability. It's even more important to consider how accurate that perception may be. What's good to know is that self-belief can be fortified and is not fixed at any one time. When riders develop a healthy level of self-belief, they also develop more confidence, resilience and emotional balance.

Your innate level of self-belief, stemming from your core beliefs, was probably already established before you were 7 years old. As we have discussed in the first chapter, these beliefs originate from your environment, genetics, people you grew up with, your early years' experiences and early school life.

Many sports coaches, equestrians and sports psychology experts will tell you that these deep beliefs cannot be changed. However, they can. The plasticity of our brains and thinking style can always be changed, with a little work.

Very often, beliefs change as circumstances change and as we age and become increasingly independent, with a different set of friends and fellow equestrians. Beliefs can also change *if* you feel that a certain belief is holding you back. We'll look at changing beliefs in a later chapter.

Self-belief is key to self-confidence. A hand equation to demonstrate this is:

Self-confidence = self-belief x experience

This means that we can improve our sporting self-confidence by enhancing our self-belief and/or the way we label our experiences. The experience may come from

- Lessons
- Schooling
- Competing
- Feedback
- What others say or do
- Recent past and present experiences (these may be horse-related or not)
- Any more distant experience that continues to run through your mind (horse and non-horse-related)

Some riders will be glass-half-empty and spend too much time on self-criticism and completely miss the importance of the learning process and all the steps forward they are making. Others are glass-half-full and see only the good, without a need to address weaknesses or learning points.

FEEDBACK TYPES

How we label, i.e., the words we choose, the picture we see in our mind's eye and the feeling we have about a particular ride all add to the experience.

Additionally, experience may come from what others say. We've already mentioned that some people need external feedback and others internal feedback. If you can only judge whether you're doing a really good job by what others say, you'll need to have a support person who backs you and can give you truthful feedback to help you to continue to improve.

If, on the other hand, you prefer internal feedback, i.e., feedback from yourself, you have to make especially sure that you aren't overly critical, judgemental or lacking in perspective.

Consider the following questions to understand your 'experience' side of the equation more:

1. If someone criticises you, do you take to heart what others say about your riding or can you easily brush it off?
2. Do you listen to others? Whom do you listen to? Are you selective? Do you admire and respect those you listen to?

3. Are there people whom you think it would be best not to listen to? Who, specifically?

4. Do you listen more to your own advice or more to the advice of others? How does this work for you? Should you listen to yourself/others more or less?

5. If you changed whom you got your best advice from (i.e., more from yourself or more from others), what would happen? What wouldn't happen?

If you are a rider's supporter, consider how you can enhance the 'experience' part of the equation.

For example,

- Preparation – can you help the rider in their preparation? This may not be hands-on coaching, but can you make sure that they are prepared, as is their horse for what they want to do? For example, if the rider is going to a competition, could you help to make up a checklist, help in loading the horse or offer to clean tack?

- Environment – is the environment for the rider enthusiastic, can-do, supportive and positive? Can you create an environment where every small success is celebrated?

- Training culture - is this positive, enthusiastic and full of belief? Imagine for a moment being the rider. How do they feel going to their lesson, clinic or competition? Can you put yourself in their shoes,

with all the unpredictability of a horse to manage
and the strong wanting to do well?

The most powerful experience a rider can have is a win. Whether that's a personal goal achieved (e.g., taking part) or winning the red rosette, the rush of feel-good chemicals gushing around the nervous system is palpable! The 'win' doesn't have to be big, celebrating small wins is a critical means of adding to 'experience' and building on self-confidence. By putting a few wins together, enough momentum is created to spur the rider on. With enough 'wins', a lacklustre day can be shrugged off and the rider has banked enough positive to stave off a loss of self-belief and self-confidence.

EXPECTATIONS

You can set goals and intentions, but have you considered your expectations? What are your expectations of each ride, each lesson and each competition you enter? If you have enjoyed a certain amount of success, has that added to your motivation or led to complacency and disappointment?

Expectations can be flexible or strict terms that you unconsciously agree to. For example, an expectation of getting a better result when competing: is that too restrictive (I must have a clear round/more than 70% in my dressage) or is it realistic (I must aim to have a clear round, although 4-8 faults are ok if the track is built up or we haven't competed in a while/I must aim for more than 70% in my dressage, although

60% may be good on the day if we're using it as a training session).

Expectations are the minimum standard we think we should achieve. Notice the word 'should'. Whenever you hear yourself or others saying 'should' or 'must', it's a firm expectation, a rule inside our minds. Notice too that the rule may be unrealistic and might harm your confidence.

Instead of expectations, aim to think more of objectives. These are manageable mini-goals for the ride on that particular day. A rider who is perfecting some part of their performance is very rarely one who feels the weight of expectation upon them. And that is a huge burden lifted from their shoulders!

Remember to set goals that are under your control. If something happens during a ride which is unexpected and uncontrollable, then learn to re-set your goal for that day accordingly. Inflexible goals and high expectations can put undue pressure on you and deplete your confidence.

REMOVING WHAT HOLDS YOU BACK

Several mental processes can hold you back from your goals and your motivation. These include:

- Self-limiting beliefs and doubts
- Procrastination
- Anxiety / low confidence
- Fear of failure

Let's address each one and find out how to remove these blocks.

SELF-LIMITING BELIEFS AND DOUBTS

All riders encounter self-limiting beliefs and self-doubt. You may have thoughts such as

- I'm not good enough
- I'm not good enough for my horse
- Other people can do it, but I can't
- I doubt I could ride any better
- I think about a fall/accident/incident all the time
- When I see other people in my class, I feel inferior

The interesting thing about these types of limiting beliefs is that the beliefs may not even be your own. What we mean by that is that your mind has magnified a certain situation or comment and made it into a belief, which is probably not true.

- Beliefs are usually picked up from others
- We borrow beliefs from the media, social media and the internet
- Our actions often depend on beliefs that may have been started many years ago
- Your limiting belief may have nothing to do with riding! It may simply appear when you ride!

Think of one belief that is holding you back. The most common self-limiting belief is not feeling good enough, you may want to start there. Let's work to get rid of that belief. Get a notepad or piece of paper and begin to write down your answers to the following questions. It's best if you write your answers by hand because it's slow! Thinking about your answers or typing them is much faster and doesn't usually allow the mind to show you its insights.

As you write, unburden yourself of your thoughts and keep writing until you're sure you've said everything. Set aside at least an hour to do this. If you complete it within an hour, go back, look over your answers and add more detail.

1. Although you feel like this belief is true, would others say it was true? If not, why not?
2. Where did this belief begin? Do remember a specific time or a rough time?
3. Was there an earlier time, maybe childhood or when you thought this way too?
4. Was the time you're thinking of to do with horses or something else?
5. What happened?
6. Does that event have any link with what you believe about yourself now?
7. How do you feel about that old event now? Was it a one-off?
8. Can you find a reason behind what happened – can you STOP thinking that way now?

9. Is it part of a pattern, something that set this thinking in motion, is the original event even valid now?
10. What would happen if you could STOP thinking in this limiting way?

Set aside time for each of your limiting beliefs about yourself and any doubts and repeat the exercise. In time, these beliefs will begin to fade, as they were probably set up at a very young age, where you did your best and couldn't have done better or events that are no longer relevant to you now.

PROCRASTINATION

Procrastination is the opposite of motivation. They both have to do with how much we prioritise something. Few people need help with getting motivated to do something they love! Many people need help to do something they dislike or see no point in doing.

Procrastination usually develops for one of two reasons

1. You don't want to do it. In this case, question whether the riding or type of riding is what you want. Horse ownership and riding make huge demands on our time, money and effort. Do you want to pause, take a break or carry on?!
2. You're anxious about doing it. Read back over the section on 'Getting in focus'. There are lots of tips about reducing your nerves and anxiety.

ANXIETY AND FEAR OF FAILURE

Anxiety can mean fixating on the negatives more than the positives. When we visited 'focus', we said to focus on what you want to happen, not what you don't want to happen. If your anxiety goes unchecked, it can lead to a fear of failure. This is added pressure on all athletes, including riders. Once again, for tips on how to reduce anxiety, see the 'Getting in focus' section.

Fear of failure is a specific anxiety that is usually caused by a lack of confidence in your own ability. Have an open and frank chat with your instructor or trainer, what do they think? Would riding at a lower level for a competition or clinic help you to regain confidence?

The fear of failure shouldn't be confused with the normal nerves that you may have before a competition, lesson or clinic. These pre-ride jitters can be re-named – in fact they should be re-named! The feelings that you have in your body are the same as if you were excited! Excitement gives you those self-same feelings and by habit, we name them 'nerves' or 'anxiety'. What would happen if you reframed it by naming those feelings as excitement? Try it!

REMEMBER TO DO THE FOLLOWING:

- Focus on the task, not the score, placing or outcome
- Ride like you don't care about the score, placing or outcome! Over-ride any negative self-talk with, "I don't care how I do today"
- Smile! This may seem an odd thing to do. But your mind associates a smile with happiness and just by smiling you can start to feel happier.

BUBBLE EXERCISE – THE CONTROLLABLE AND UNCONTROLLABLE

Draw two circles, one inside the other in the middle of a piece of paper. The inner circle is your mind; in that circle write down the things you can control e.g., how you react, your position, timing, accuracy, rhythm etc. Around the outer circle write down what you can't control e.g., other competitors, other riders' results, spectators, the weather, judges etc.

Now focus on improving the things you can control in the middle.

8

CAUSE AND EFFECT

People can be either 'at-cause' or 'at-effect'. Being at-effect is a state of powerlessness. It's when someone blames everyone and everything outside of themselves. People who are extremely at-effect will look first to something outside of themselves to find excuses and reasons. Their attention is very much placed on the external world, they are looking to the outside, not inside of themselves.

When people are at-cause, they look first to themselves. How did X happen? How can I make sure it doesn't happen again or that I improve and do it better? This is a place of empowerment because a person at cause believes they can alter their outcome.

A person at cause tends to get results; a person at effect tends to get reasons. Which side would you rather be on?

At cause > At effect

If we make sure that we are more on the cause side of the equation, we gain flexibility and in turn, more control. Our thinking stems from inside us and is less affected by the outside. It's a much more stoic way of being. It's also far more powerful and resilient. If something negative happens, such as a knocked down pole in jumping, we don't blame the horse, the showground or anyone else, we look to how we could do that self-same jump, in the exact same circumstances, differently.

If we're on the at-effect side of the equation, we are at the mercy of our environment and all the people and horses in it. It's an outside-in mode of thinking. For example, if our horse goes lame, we would find it very difficult to not be frustrated, fed up and looking instantly to blame the horse (did he/she career around the paddock?) or the farrier or another horse or anyone else who was near to the horse. A more empowering way of thinking is how can I prevent this in the future or if my horse is lame, what is the best recovery strategy or how I can make the most of this by spending more time grooming or in-hand grazing?

Not only does the at-cause mindset protect you from reacting and overreacting or being disproportionately emotional, but it also protects you from anxiety, depression, stress and excessive frustration in future circumstances. It's like banking a little resilience and building mental toughness.

WAYS TO KEEP TO THE AT-CAUSE SIDE OF THE EQUATION

Being at cause 100% of the time isn't always achievable! It's aspirational! It is always good to be able to have the mental strength to draw upon when needed. In trying situations, remember your mindset is to be protected!

You can ask yourself these questions about past issues or ones that are happening now:

1. What practical measures can I take to make this situation better/easier?
2. What can I learn from this?
3. Is it helpful to my emotional state to blame other people / other things?
4. Is my reaction proportionate? Am I overreacting?
5. How can I make this into a learning experience?

If these questions don't do the trick, try this visualisation. Imagine yourself watching the situation unfold. Now take yourself up to the ceiling and watch from there; how does being above the situation make you feel? If you need to, why not go to sky-scraper height and look down and observe the situation from this greater height?

Now, how do you feel?

9

TRIGGERS

Triggers can be good or bad – they can set off positive, empowering responses and behaviours, or they can do exactly the opposite. Knowing what triggers, you and how to either remove or dampen the effects of that negative trigger and make the most of positive triggers is very useful in sport.

A trigger can be something we see, touch, hear or an action we do. This may ultimately bring on a certain emotion or action.

Knowing your negative triggers, minimising them or eradicating them can prevent them from becoming the horse's triggers too.

Before we start to remove specific triggers, we need to know what they are. Think about how your mind knows it's time to feel nervous/anxious/frustrated/disappointed/negative.

Here's an example: having a lesson – we're aiming to pinpoint the specific moment that the nerves start. We're then going to think about whether it was the sight, sound or touch of something or some action you started that sparked your response. If you think, "It's just the thought of it!" Then what are you seeing, hearing or doing in your head?

Do you feel triggered...

- Before the lesson – when? The day before? An hour before? When do you arrive at the yard? When your instructor arrives? When you see your horse, bridle, saddle or stable?
- As you mount? Is it just as you get on or when you adjust the girth, pick up the reins or start to walk?
- As you warm up? When you walk, trot, canter, begin to school on the flat or over a jump? Does the jump have to be a certain height?
- During the lesson – what are you doing, seeing or hearing for your mind to know it's time to feel bad?

Think about when you are triggered to be anything other than positive! Then consider what is the specific trigger.

Once you have an idea of the trigger, you can try these techniques to get rid of it. The first technique is used to get a particularly triggering thought out of your mind. The second works on what-ifs and is also good for those disaster movies we run through our minds – thinking about all the things that could go wrong.

1. SWISH PATTERN

This is a technique that's quick and easy to do and removes specific triggers, as well as confusion, anxiety, frustration, disappointment, worries and doubts. The Swish Pattern is a confusion technique: if you get confused, you're doing it right!

A good idea is to have someone read out the instructions step by step or, record the instructions for yourself with pauses so that you can do the technique without having to read the steps.

1. When you think of your trigger situation, do you have a picture in your head? Make sure you are not watching yourself, but that you're actually in the picture.

2. This is your old picture. Seal it in with a click of the fingers or clap of your hands.

3. Now, think about your ideal way of doing things. Do you have a picture of this? *This picture will be very much the same as the old picture; you are still riding, it's the same horse and same location. Your horse is acting in the same way. What will be different is how you react.*

4. Imagine you have a remote control, like a television remote and can adjust the colours, brightness and focus of this second picture. Use your remote control

to change these until they are just perfect for you and the picture looks attractive.

5. Think about the sounds (if any)..... people's voices, your inner voice, your horse's footfall....you could even have another imaginary sound, like your favourite music; turn up the loudness of the sounds.

6. Now notice the feelings, let's turn up all the wonderful positive feelings, confidence, enthusiasm, joy, determination and calmness. Imagine you have a dial turning up to 10. Turn up the feelings, making them stronger and stronger and the dial is turning up to 10.

7. Now step out of the picture, so that you can see yourself in the picture. Seal this picture in with a click of your fingers. Let's call this your new picture.

8. (Fast:) Put the old picture up on the screen, big and bright. New picture lower left-hand corner, small and dark (see diagram 1 below). In a moment, when you think of the word 'Swish!' the new picture will explode up to cover the old picture. The old picture will fade away (see diagram 2 below).

Diagram 1   Diagram 2

9. OK, So now Swish! Open your eyes, close your eyes

10. (Speak fast for this step): Put the old picture up on the screen, big and bright. New picture lower left-hand corner, small and dark. In a moment, when you think of the word 'Swish!' the new picture will explode up to cover the old picture. The old picture will fade away.

11. OK, So now Swish! Open your eyes, close your eyes

12. (Speak fast for this step): Put the old picture up on the screen, big and bright. New picture lower left-hand corner, small and dark. In a moment, when you think of the word 'Swish!' the new picture will explode up to cover the old picture. The old picture will fade away.

13. OK, So now Swish! Open your eyes, close your eyes

14. (Speak fast for this step): Put the old picture up on the screen, big and bright. New picture lower left-hand corner, small and dark. In a moment, when you think

of the word 'Swish!' the new picture will explode up to cover the old picture. The old picture will fade away.

15. OK, So now Swish! Open your eyes, close your eyes

16. (Speak fast for this step): Put the old picture up on the screen, big and bright. New picture lower left-hand corner, small and dark. In a moment, when you think of the word 'Swish!' the new picture will explode up to cover the old picture. The old picture will fade away.

17. OK, So now Swish! Open your eyes, close your eyes

18. (Speak fast for this step): Put the old picture up on the screen, big and bright. New picture lower left-hand corner, small and dark. In a moment, when you think of the word 'Swish!' the new picture will explode up to cover the old picture. The old picture will fade away.

19. Repeat the Swishing until can't get the old picture back.

20. OK, So now Swish! Open your eyes, keep your eyes open

21. How do you feel about that old trigger and issue now?!

What usually happens: the old picture fades or disappears and the negative emotions go with it.

Swish is an excellent technique to do for 5 minutes per day on a particular fear, frustration, worry or other bad feelings. It's also perfect if something doesn't go to plan, e.g., you're riding and your horse spooks or you're in a warm-up and you make a mistake, Swish it away before it plays on your mind – in this case, it's super as a re-set button!

2. REWIND

Similarly, to the Swish Pattern, Rewind is a confusion technique. It's perfect for what-if movies that may play on an incessant loop in your mind.

1.   Ask yourself, on a score of 0-10, 0 being a nonentity and 10 being a full-blown phobia, how do you rate your discomfort?

2.   Design a quick movie (5-10 seconds long). Have the first and last frames/scenes be where you feel safe and calm. You could be at home relaxing or you could be away from anything to do with horses. In the middle section, add in your what-ifs, just skip from scene to scene, to keep it quick.

3.   Now picture being in a cinema. Sit as close to the screen as your fear allows, and move towards the back seats or even into the projector booth if you find that more comfortable.

4.   Put the first frame of your movie on the screen, on pause. Make it black and white.

5.   (Speak fast for this step): Run the movie forward, black & white at normal speed, watching yourself on screen.

CLAIRE NIXON-ORD UKCC LEVEL 4 COACH & TRACEY COLE BSC, PHD

6. Imagine floating out of your cinema seat and right into the cinema screen, so that you're in the movie.

7. (Speak fast for this step): Put the last frame of the movie on the screen. Make it in colour. Run the movie backwards in colour, with you in the movie, at 2x normal speed.

8. When you reach the start of the movie, repeat as before:

9. (Speak fast for this step): Put the first frame of your movie on the screen, on pause. Make it black and white.
10. (Speak fast for this step): Run the movie forward, black & white at normal speed, watching yourself on screen.

11. Imagine floating out of your cinema seat and right into the cinema screen, so that you're in the movie.

12. You'll repeat going forwards and backwards and on each backwards run, make the movie go even faster at 4x, 5x, 10x, 20x, 50x, and 100x normal speed.

13. Repeat starting from step 1 until fears and what-ifs have gone.

What usually happens: the movie becomes more difficult to recall; often the first and last frames remain and the rest of the movie is no longer as accessible.

TROUBLESHOOTING THESE TWO TECHNIQUES

1. I can't see pictures very clearly. That's not a problem, simply have on your 'mental screen' the best pictures you can have. They may be grey, grainy and unfocused, but that doesn't matter.

2. My fear or nerves go when I do the technique, but return when I'm actually riding. This means that your mind hasn't fully embedded the new way of thinking and the old way of thinking is still stronger. Practise one or both techniques every day for about 5-10 minutes.

3. I'd like to do these techniques before I ride, but I feel too nervous or frustrated to do them! Make sure you're practising at home when you're away from the stables. Practise when you aren't planning to ride. Practise for 5-10 minutes every day. That way, you'll be able to do the technique more and more easily and automatically just before your ride.

4. I forget the instructions and have to read what to do, this interrupts the technique. Have someone read the instructions to you or record them for yourself and

play them back on your phone. You'll soon remember all the instructions!

POSITIVE TRIGGERS

Knowing what your cues are to feel good is a means of gaining independence. It's important to be able to see each ride as either purely for pleasure and/or as a learning experience. As the saying goes, you're either winning or you're learning. Both are hugely positive. It's accepting this that is the difference that makes the difference.

We don't tell ourselves that we've done well often enough. Besides the negative voice inside your head, the inner critic, there is also a positive one (sometimes) struggling to be heard!

Two powerful positive triggers that you can use to gain perspective and move on are to use a type of pat on the back admission of having done well in some respect and secondly, to be grateful for the opportunity.

1. The pat on the back

Remember that equestrianism is not only a physical sport, it's highly mental in mature too. Giving yourself a 'pat on the back', finding a positive and telling yourself you did well, keeps your mind in a healthier and stronger state. Saying it to yourself, inside your head, at least 3-5 times and meaning it, will ensure you stay more balanced. "I did well when I did X" or "I did well to learn X." Nobody is saying that after a disappointing ride that it's easy to eke out a positive, but that it is a means of working with your mind that will reap benefits.

2. Gratitude

Research[1] has shown that being grateful enhances performance, lowers stress, and improves confidence, happiness and goal-getting. Gratitude also helps us to become more patient and less likely to feel overly judgemental and angry with ourselves.

You can write down 5 (or more) things you are grateful for each day. Or, you can say them to yourself. When you begin to add the people, horses, opportunities, as well as simple things like having good food to eat, clean water to drink and a cosy bed to sleep in, naming 5 things is never difficult!

If you'd like to power up the gratitude, why not name 5 things every hour? It makes a real difference to your perspective.

https://www.researchgate.net/publication/333710843_Gratitude_in_Sport_Positive_Psychology_for_Athletes_and_Implications_for_Mental_Health_Well-Being_and_Performance

10

VISUALISATIONS

I n sport, it is important to look at and watch other sports. For athletes, the use of visualisation is really important, so that they can see what they are going to do. E.g., skiers, and Formula One drivers visualise their turns and sports like gymnastics or diving their routines. We can use these powerful visualisations in equestrian sports for dressage tests, and show jumping rounds (especially jumping jumps you may not like e.g., spreads, water trays and certain colours of jumps like rainbow poles). Cross-country courses after you've walked the course (taking photos of the jumps as you walk around) help you remember which way you are turning or the lines you are taking.

If you have a certain phobia or fear of e.g., a type or colour of the jump. Then both Tracey or I can help you with a personalised script which we can record for you to listen to help you overcome your fear. Details of how to get in touch are in the about the authors in the back of this book.

Athletes also are seen with headphones on maybe they are listening to their favourite playlist, or their spoken routine e.g., dressage test, show jumping course turns etc.

Before you start your visualisations, it is important to regulate your breathing to help get you into a state of flow to help you stay calm and in control of your emotions.

11

SELF-CARE

I n the equestrian industry, there seems to be a culture whereby if you take time off work, you are classified as lazy or if you are injured there is pressure for you to be back to work ASAP, rather than focusing on your recovery. If you fall off and get straight back on your horse, you're awarded an imaginary badge of bravery. Now I'm not saying all yards are like this, but I have found myself feeling the pressure to be back up and running after an injury.

Is this because we all strive to wear an invisible badge to fit in, whether it's a badge of honour for bravery, a badge for hard work or on the flip side we are awarded a badge for being lazy, for not working hard enough. We can't win, can we?

If we continue down this road, are we heading for burnout? Burnout is now classified as a state of mental, physical and emotional exhaustion caused by unmanaged stress. As equestrians, we can have a stressful job working with horses and people who can be demanding and unpredictable. You may be suffering without even knowing you have the extreme symptoms of not being able to function normally, feeling drained, unable to cope, and lacking energy.

If we have learnt anything from the global pandemic, then surely it is how important our mental and physical health is. So, what can we do to help ourselves? If you think of your body and mind as your mobile phone, if you keep using your mobile without recharging then your battery will die and therefore you can't use it. How many times do you forget to charge your phone? How many times do you allow yourself to recharge your batteries?

It's time we act now to enable ourselves to recharge our batteries without feeling guilty for taking time out. If we think about it differently, what happens if you take a break to do something for yourself? What happens?

For me, I come back feeling refreshed with energy, almost a skip in my step and I show up as my best version of myself ready to coach or ride. Every lesson you have you want to feel like you've got enough energy so that you can ride to your best ability.

What does self-care look like? Well, think about the things which make you happy. What do you love doing? And write them down.

- Spending time with loved ones and friends and making memories.

- Going for walks in the countryside, running, going to the gym, competing yourself or even having training just for you or other sports.
- Going to get beauty treatments, going to a spa or your hair done.
- Spending time doing a hobby, going shopping or going to watch a film.
- Taking time out in the garden or in the sun to listen to the birds.

There are so many things you could choose from I've not exhausted the list. Choose one thing once a week or once a month, whatever works for you that you want to do.

We also need to look after our physical health which also includes getting plenty of quality hours of sleep, less screen time before bed, drinking plenty of water, eating the right foods and fitness levels. Now, this sounds straightforward but I know it is easy to fall into the wrong habits when we are tired. As we can grab the wrong foods e.g., a chocolate bar (short-term energy solution) compared to a banana (slower release of healthy energy). I know when I'm on the go I will drink more water if it comes out of the fridge chilled with a slice of lemon which is my personal preference but find out what you prefer.

For our mental health, we need to set our boundaries e.g., when sponsors or owners can contact us and can expect a reply, rather than 24/7. To allow us to take time away from our screens.

Some people believe in listening to meditation recordings. These can be positive mindset meditations for confidence or releasing your limiting beliefs.

12

UNLOCK YOUR BEST
PERFORMANCE IN THE RING

Before you get to a competition preparation is key. If you're a list-writing person that's great. Then you can write your list of everything you need to take with you. Include your times, and give yourself extra time, so you're not rushing on the day.

When you're making a plan, work backwards from the competition date and include everything you need to practice. This can include arena hires to practice in a different environment.

Dealing with pressure – "don't panic".

It is vital that you can cope with pressure, as there will be times working with horses and people you will feel under pressure, whether it's to be on time or even to perform.

Make sure if something doesn't go to plan, don't panic, take a deep breath, and use the space around you so that you can react the way you want to.

If at a competition something bothers you before the competition have the conversation e.g. if it's something someone does or says to you then remind them to try not to do the action. This will help with clear boundaries and communications.

If you haven't done much competition then when you're at home it's a good idea to practise riding in your competition gear, so that you can relax and feel comfortable in the clothing you are wearing. Make sure you run through your dressage tests, so you know it inside out which will help take the pressure off.

In your planning with your coach (we always recommend using a qualified registered coach, so that they are up to date with current industry practices and CPD). See what is available in the local area from test riding clinics, dressage online competitions, clinics, and other coaches who can support the same goals you have.

Listen to the language you are using, if it is negative words, you are using look at how you can reframe them. E.g., I hate jumping purple spreads > I love show jumping focusing on my rhythm.

If you feel like this is an area in which you would like more support, please contact either of us to help support you.

PART III

SUPPORTERS - CHEERLEADERS

In this section, you will gain top tips on how to best support riders.

13

YOUR IMPACT ON OTHERS

A positive impact on your rider is priceless. The more positive your input, the more enjoyment the rider takes from their sport. Additionally, a positive involvement can result in greater motivation, self-confidence and self-esteem. These qualities often become transferable to other aspects of life too.

A negative response from your rider could add pressure and result in them underachieving or giving up their equestrianism.

It's a fine line between being involved and being overly involved. Whilst trying to be kind and supportive, an overly-involved supporter can lead to the supporter riding vicariously through the rider or inflating the rider's expectations.

At this stage, it's vital that the rider enjoys riding as their number one aim. External pressure can gnaw away at enjoyment.

VALUES, PREFERENCES (METAPROGRAMS) AND BELIEFS

In the opening part of this book, we looked at your values, beliefs and preferences (metaprograms). It would be invaluable for you to answer the questions and review them with your rider. Not only is it quite good fun to understand how different people filter differently, but it will also give you a huge insight into how your rider's mind works, how they like information to be passed on to them (are they a carrot or a stick person or a little of both) and whether they need external feedback or external support.

After comparing preferences, do the same exercises for values and beliefs and review yours and your riders. This will give you a lot of information about the make-up of their personality as a rider. You may think that you know them really well, but often this reveals surprises and knowledge is power!

PERCEPTIONS

Having a balanced, realistic perception of the rider, their potential and their own goals goes a long way to backing them in a healthy and non-intrusive way. How we make a perception is an interesting one to consider.

- Do you and your rider share the same perceptions of them, their riding and their goals?
- Do you and your rider unpack and analyse a ride, competition, lesson or clinic in the same way? Is one of you more positive or negative?

It's not necessary to have the same perceptions as someone else, as perceptions are very personal and as individual as a fingerprint. What's important is to understand how we process an event and how we act because of it.

We perceive what's happening through our five senses. We take an enormous amount of information into our brains every second – estimated at between 11 million and 2 billion pieces of information per second. We can't begin to organise that amount of data every second!

The brain uses a filtering system to cut down information into a more manageable amount.

How we filter the information is not only personal to us but can alter our perceptions radically. For example, in simplistic terms, we may filter as glass-half-empty people or glass-half-full people.

The first set of filters deletes, distorts and generalises the mass of information.

- Deletion – we delete what we think is of little importance. A pessimistic rider may delete all the times something went well (this is why it's good to journal after a lesson, ride or competition!). A more optimistic one may delete the errors and mistakes (is this rider deleting areas to improve upon?).

- Distortion – we may make mountains out of molehills or molehills out of mountains
- Generalisation – you often hear this in people's words. E.g., every, never, all, everyone, nobody. As a negative, it means we over-generalise and make sweeping statements about our ability or the success of the ride. We push away the times we did something right or had a great training session.

Apart from these filters, there's a host of others to distil the incoming descriptions about what's happening even more. E.g., the filters we have already met such as preferences, beliefs and values, but also our memories and attitudes.

The information is finally grouped into 5-9 pieces of information.

It's hard to imagine that of the 11 million – 2 billion pieces of information per second that hit our brains, we retain only 5-9 chunked-together pieces. There's an incredible loss of information going on!

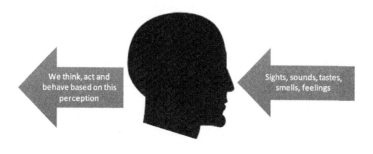

5-9 chunks of information that we're aware of

Extensive filtering

11 million pieces of information per second

Knowing this, how can we ever be sure of any of our perceptions? Aren't all perceptions woefully inadequate?

Can you imagine the amount of editing that has occurred? How much that is left behind, in our minds, is accurate?

This is the reason why two people having the same experience may describe it in totally different ways. It's also why a rider and a supporter may not agree on whether the ride was a good one or one to identify weaknesses.

As a rider or supporter, it's good if we can recover what that mind has deleted, distorted or generalised on, to give us a more rounded point of view. Here are some questions that might highlight where we filter out important events. This table is also available as a PDF at https://www.traceycolenlp.com/**riders-unlock-your-riding-success**/

Rider Statement	Support Retort/Question
I **never** get it right	**Never**? What would happen if you did?
Everyone can do it apart from me	**Everyone**? Who do you mean, specifically?
She thinks I'm no good She thinks I'm no good because she shouts at me	How specifically do you know that? Have you ever shouted at someone you thought was quite good in some way?
I **can't** do it	You can't do it **yet**. What prevents you? What would happen if you could?
My horse makes my riding look bad	How does what your horse is doing cause you to choose to think that? How specifically does your horse do that?

Imagine now that the rider statements come from the supporter – e.g., **"You** never get it right". Unless the rider has the language to question the statement, the impact on their mind, especially over time, would be very detrimental.

DISTANT PAST EXPERIENCES

Distance from past experiences also colour our perceptions. They were also filtered in the same way as above. They may have undergone even more filtering since then, with layers of self-talk, self-criticism or self-praise.

RE-ASSESS YOUR PERCEPTIONS

If there is an uncomfortable memory that is a trigger that's changing how you think about yourself as a rider or even changing how you ride, this will be dampening your self-belief. Learn how to lessen the impact of old memories in the 'Rider' section.

YOUR TRIGGERS

Your rider's triggers and your own can be emotionally unexploded bombs! Knowing more about your rider's triggers in the 'Rider' section highlights possible ways to defuse them safely!

Did you know that humans have nerve cells called mirror neurones? These are neurones that respond equally whether you're doing a certain action or you're observing it. When you observe it, you often repeat what you're seeing – think about yawning! As soon as someone starts to yawn, you do it too! Smiling is another example.

As a supporter, you may also activate mirror neurones when you watch your rider. You feel that very deep sense of empathy and it is almost as if the unfair dressage score or unnecessary comment from a spectator is directed right at you.

Knowing whether you are triggered by other riders, be they coaches, trainers, instructors or judges when your rider receives criticism may be something to consider. Are you also triggered if your rider underperforms? Do you feel jealous if other riders perform better?

Furthermore, are you triggered into a highly negative and unhelpful state such as frustration, anger (or even rage)?

Part of being able to be supportive is not to add to the pressure and high emotional state of your rider. Knowing that you are triggered and being completely aware of what those triggers are is the first step to remaining calm and positive. Ask yourself:

- Are my triggers from my own equestrian or sporting life? Are they from my own life in general?
- Do these comments belong more to a past version of myself, that the present version of my rider?
- Am I over-reacting – is this a real perception, is this helpful?

If your comments are directed at your rider, aim to give them praise for something, no matter how subtle, that you admired or that went well. There's no need to go overboard on the praise, keep it real. Steer clear of criticism initially.

You could ask a question of your rider, "Do you want to talk about it? ", "Were you feeling a bit tired today? You did well at X" or "What was your tactic there? I could see you were trying to do X".

Some riders prefer to be quiet and internally process for themselves what has happened (see Preferences: How do you know when you're doing a good job?). After that. They may want your opinion – equally, they may not!

Other riders may process it by talking it through. In that case, listen more and talk less.

It's good to ask your rider what would be more comfortable for them so that you have the right strategy for the right rider.

PROJECTION

We often project onto others how we think they are. According to Carl Jung, we're projecting that part of ourselves onto them! Although humans have lost most of their animalistic sixth sense, we can still sense what someone believes about us. It's an unspoken communication and it is stronger than we give it credit. Sending a projection of positivity, motivation, determination, enjoyment and success is received in the same way as body language is received. Interestingly, only 7% of human communication can be attributed to words. 93% is a combination of body language and voice tonality.

Remember to project onto your rider the confident, can-do rider you want them to be! Any doubts will be conveyed, whether you verbalise them or not!

Putting yourself in their shoes – Perceptual Positions

This technique helps you to gain your rider's perspective. It's an illuminating exercise!

Choose three places to sit or stand in your room. You will move to each place as you 'become' each person. Moving position aids the success of this technique!

Position 1

In this position, you are yourself. This is you with all your opinions, ideas, hopes, goals, dreams and any criticisms of your rider

Position 2

In this position, you are now your rider. You now have all *their* opinions, ideas, hopes, goals, dreams and any criticisms of *you*!

Position 3

This person is someone who is the voice of reason, someone with a balanced point of view about you and your rider. It could be someone at home or an instructor, coach or another rider.

1. Arrange the 3 positions so that each can see the other two.
2. Go to Position 1 and look at Position 2. In your head, tell the rider all your worries, anxieties, dilemmas, doubts, hopes, dreams, goals, opinions etc. Tell the about any specific times you think are relevant. Pour it all out until you can't think of anything more.
3. Break state: this means that you think about something else. You could go on your phone for 20-30 seconds or get a drink of water.
4. Move to Position 2, the rider. Be the rider and look towards Position 1. In your head, tell position 1, i.e., you the supporter, how you feel and think about

things. Advise. Give (positive) criticism. Unload everything you have to say.

5. Break state: go on your phone for 20-30 seconds, or have a drink.

6. Move to Position 3, the observer, the voice of reason. Look at the other two positions. You have observed their commentaries, now you can give your version as the interested observer. What advice would you give to each one? What comments do you have on their situations/behaviour/thoughts?

7. Break state: go on your phone for 20-30 seconds, or have a drink

8. Go back to Position 1. How do you feel about your rider's perspective now?

You can revisit this technique frequently, it's also useful for your rider to do for themselves, in which case, they put themselves into Position 1, you into Position 2 and the observer into Position 3.

14

ENVIRONMENT

For us to thrive then we need to make sure we are in a safe environment to thrive. We need to have the following things in an environment to thrive.

1. Clear communications and boundaries.
2. Community, social groups with the right positive people and positive use of language.
3. Facilities – well maintained including access to the space we need and or jumps etc.
4. Other events, demos or clinics can also help contribute to your goals and or self-care.
5. People are friendly, knowledgeable, supportive, and helpful.
6. Within the facilities, they have affirmations or motivational quotes around to help you, especially if you're having a hard day.

Have a look at your training environment, what things make you get anxious? Mine would be anything wrong with safety or potential incidents. Does your environment support you? What can you add or change in your current environment to help best support you?

At Swinhoe Farm Riding Centre we have motivational quotes in the indoor arena (next to the mounting block – to help riders who are maybe anxious on getting on), in the toilets (this is where people normally will have quite time, where it will they gather their thoughts or where they can be tough on themselves, by them reading or subconsciously reading these quotes it often helps them in their own self-belief). This is an easy thing that you can implement on any yard, even in your trailer or wagon, so that you can remind yourself that you are good enough.

Now, have a think at what changes can you implement to help you on your way to your competition, exam and in the competition environment? Are you organised, are you listening to the right songs to help you get into the right mood? Have you got motivational quotes up? Or have you got a small whiteboard, so you can practice through your dressage test? Or cross-country course?

15

PERFORMANCE CONVERSATIONS

This chapter is aimed at coaches, parents, and riders.

Developing conversations are key to becoming a coach but also for everyone involved within the equestrian sport, which includes Parents, Riders (being able to understand what they are doing and put it into words) and other people within the equestrian world. The ability to start a conversation, control and direct the conversation but most importantly to pause and listen to the rider is so important to build up a relationship with your riders.

Now in other sports, they do a lot more performance conversations away from their equipment because it helps their athletes become focused on what they are wanting to achieve but also helps keep their mental skills too as they normally say 80% mental and 20% skill. When you hear Cristiano Ronaldo says talent alone is not enough, you must be dedicated to putting in the hard work and he says his mental skills are just as strong now as he started. Hopefully, over time we equestrians will catch up on our mental skills to help improve our performances.

Performance conversations are cycles of asking questions, pausing, and listening, double checking you have understood what they have said to you in their own words (re-framed – remembering their Representational System keywords which can add a deeper and greater understanding) and can then ask for any reflections or anything else they could add.

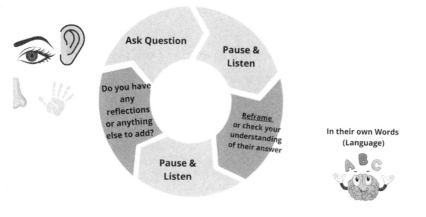

Can you think of some questions you can ask?

I think it would be beneficial to have a bank of questions for you ready to ask your riders, so here are a few to get you started. Practice on your riders on and off the horse. You can also ask friends or family members to help you practise your conversations because the more we use conversations, the better our timing becomes, the more confident we become and most importantly the greater insights our riders gain and the understandings we gain. Remember that silence is so important because it allows the riders to process their own thoughts and feelings.

START THE CONVERSATION – THINK ABOUT WHAT GOALS THEY WANT TO ACHIEVE.

- How's your week been?
- Can you tell me about you and your horse?
- What would you like to achieve?
- What is important for you to achieve?

Think of this as the chorus cycle- you repeat after each question you ask, so you are listening to your riders, so you both are on the same page.

Pause and Listen
Then reframe it back to them in their own words
Pause and Listen
Ask if they have any reflections or anything else to add.

Pause and Listen

Then reframe it back to them in their own words

Pause and Listen

Ask if they have any reflections or anything else to add.

ACHIEVEMENT AND SUCCESS

- What does that look like to you?
- How would it feel to achieve?
- How will you know you have achieved?
- What does success mean to you?

Repeat chorus cycle

Thought Process

- **How are you going to achieve this?**
- **What small steps can you take to achieve this?**

Repeat chorus cycle

Action Plan

- What one thing do you need to focus on first?
- Is there anything you know you need to work on to build your strengths?
- Is there anything that will or could prevent you from achieving?
- How can you overcome that?

Repeat chorus cycle

Reflect and Review

- How does it feel to talk about your goals?
- What action are you going to take first?
- What has been your biggest incite?

Repeat chorus cycle

ANY REFLECTIONS?

That's great we now have a Plan/Goal/Strategy!

Really important - to write this down!

To become a reality!

16

BE THE NUMBER 1 SUPPORTER - HOW TO SUPPORT YOUR RIDER

There are several ways that a rider and their supporter can encourage and optimise this journey together. Here are some ideas of what to do and what to avoid.

LEARNING OPPORTUNITIES FOR THE RIDER

Make opportunities for the rider to learn by doing. Although riders can learn by watching others and listening to supporters, instructors and others, the best way for them to learn is to ride more. Little and often, with bitesize chunks of focused practice.

Sometimes, riders will learn more by figuring it out for themselves. Testing an idea that may or not work. This is a great way to learn, not only because it enhances problem-solving, but it can also build stronger resilience. Having had this type of practice when outside of a competition or pressurised situation, gives the rider a chance to explore making mistakes and correcting them in the moment. The very best riders can make minute adjustments moment-to-moment when things don't go exactly to plan.

Being exposed to non-ideal conditions helps us to become even better riders. This means allowing mistakes to happen, so the rider is more aware and more able to modify their riding naturally.

FOCUS

If your rider has moments of anxiety or doubt, one reminder is to 'focus on what you want'. Anxiety is a reminder from the unconscious mind that someone has their focus fixed on the negatives. Thinking of anxiety as an alarm to tell us to stop it can help!

Focus and staying in the now needs practice but reaps so many benefits. Thus, consistency, routine and structure can improve focus. Controlling the controllable and defocusing on those things outside of our control – again this comes with increasing the learning opportunities and maintaining focus.

MENTAL REHEARSAL AND VISUALISATION

Practising with your rider may be easier than them visualising alone. Use a script, write a script (will lots of imagery, sights, sounds, feelings and smells). Remind your rider to feel the motion; to know the position of the arms, legs, hands and head; to feel the muscle contractions in the leg as they visualise a turn or bend; to feel their hands and to consider their posture. The more real the visualisation feels the better. The rider could be sitting astride a Swiss ball or be on the arm of a sturdy armchair, they could have the reins in their hands!

BRAIN TRAINING

It would be ideal if you could run through the Swish Pattern and Rewind techniques with them (in the Triggers chapter). Having someone read each step of the instructions makes it easier and sets you up for more success! These techniques work best if repeated frequently and that would mean doing about 5-10 minutes each day until they aren't needed.

Another key thing to keep track of is your rider's self-talk. Chat to your rider about what happens inside their head, what do they tell themselves? (Ask until you're convinced, they have told you what they really tell themselves). Work through a Pattern Interrupt together (see the Getting in focus chapter).

If your rider has more major self-doubts, self-limiting beliefs and negative emotions such as fear, guilt, regret etc. Do explore using Time Line Therapy® with a qualified practitioner who specialises in equestrianism.

GOALS

Goals give direction, it's useful to have both processes- (e.g., one small 'set-piece') and performance- (e.g., results) related goals.

As a rider and supporter, goal setting will become second nature. Setting goals that are both longer-term and shorter-term is a means of weekly or monthly ones will uphold the focus, whilst sustaining an ethos of moving forwards.

You can support your rider by enabling some small goals to be easily achievable to maintain an optimistic outlook and a degree of success. Furthermore, a rider can begin to feel like the balance has swung in favour of self-confidence, self-belief and a can-do attitude. This is incredibly empowering when going through the ups and downs of horse ownership, riding and competing.

One final word about goals, don't take goals to competitions or clinics. Set the goals for the training! You can set results-oriented goals, however, don't lose focus on the riding. A rider who has the end goal in mind can be blinded and distracted from their performance. Encourage your rider to leave the goals behind for one day and concentrate on the task.

FEEDBACK

Riders may take feedback too personally. That's where a supporter can help the rider to disassociate from the advice and see it more in the cold light of day. This, however, needs practice!

As a supporter, you may want to create a habit of breaking down a coach's feedback sandwich – what went well, what is there to learn/improve upon and what is the overall positive from the experience? The latter is a time for a mental pat on the back!

When receiving feedback from a coach – suggest to your rider that they

avoid being defensive; this is difficult but worthwhile in boosting resilience and accepting feedback as a positive. The rider should thank the coach for their help.

COMPLEMENTARY STRATEGIES

Many practices work hand in hand to aid the rider's mental and physical well-being. You may want to suggest ways to help your rider find relaxation, calmness and balance.

1. Music – a good way to reset the mind and bring calm or focus. Think about the music you play on the way to an event. Does your rider prefer something energising and upbeat? Calming and soothing? Music on the way home from an event could be useful in this regard too.
2. EquiPilates™, Franklin Method® and yoga – these exercise regimens aid physical and mental focus, proprioception and suppleness, as well as mental relaxation. There are many rider-centred groups that you can join on Facebook or Zoom.
3. Deep breathing and breathing techniques – some trainers advocate breathing out as you ride a downward transition and breathing in as you transition upwards. In addition, your rider can also

start a warm-up by breathing in time with the horse's stride, for example, breathe in for 4, out for 4.

Breathing is also a perfect way to find better postural stability and the ability to sit longer and stronger in the saddle, as well as a quick and easy way to dispel nerves.

Being more aware of your breathing and breathing correctly, using a greater lung capacity, and feeling as if you were breathing deeply into your pelvis, helps you to be able to move more with your horse.

Here are two unmounted exercises to try with your rider.

BOX BREATHING

1. Breathe in whilst counting to 4 slowly.
2. Hold your breath for a count of 4.
3. Exhale slowly whilst counting to 4.
4. Repeat.

You can practise imagining that you are sending the breath into your tummy, pelvis or toes and notice how each feels.

Lion's roar

This is a yoga technique. You could go into the lion pose or simply sit in a comfortable position. It's perfect for releasing stress and tension. Practise with your rider and have a giggle!

1. Inhale through your nose.
2. Look upwards and stick out your tongue towards your chin.
3. Exhale, making the sound of a lion's roar.

SOME DOS AND DON'TS

Do

- Accept they may not win every time.
- Allow them to be a child/teenager/young adult and have fun.
- Encourage other sports interests too, these can be distractions or can aid in physical training – other sports can improve coordination, balance, speed of movement, strength and rhythm.
- Remain calm and relaxed for lessons clinics and competitions.
- Encourage downtime away from horses.
- Reassure that you are always there for them.
- Resist the temptation to coach your own child, it may not work! Get an instructor, coach or trainer.
- Encourage kindness, selflessness, gratitude and sharing within the sport.

- Be aware that riders often plateau after reaching a certain level and may need time to adjust before moving upwards again.
- Understand that as a rider leaves their comfort zone, (e.g., trying out a new discipline or going up the levels) it can feel immensely uncomfortable. Encourage your rider to look back over how far they have come.
- Praise efforts such as learning something new, tenacity and trying hard.
- Support their coach, trainer or instructor, this will decrease any confusing instructions given by both parties.
- Encourage the rider to develop self-awareness of their physical and mental abilities, to improve self-confidence.

Don't

- Be the constant equestrian parent, whether at the breakfast table or around the television and allow your rider to switch off.
- Define your rider as only a rider.
- Reward successes with over-blown gifts, and give small simple rewards – rewarding with your time is great.
- Guilt-trip your rider – "Do you know how much this all costs?"
- Do everything for them – they can plan and manage themselves more and more as they get older.

- Compare your rider with others – whether comparing positively or negatively!
- Spend proportionally more time with the rider than any other children you may have.
- Disagree with the coach and give different advice – instead, chat with the coach and ask more about their methods.
- Forget that riding is meant to be fun! Your rider should be enjoying their riding life, any additional pressures may take the enjoyment away.

ABOUT THE AUTHOR

CLAIRE NIXON-ORD

Claire is a highly qualified equestrian coach, author, guest speaker and entrepreneur based in Northumberland. She overcame all barriers to work up to the top of the equestrian industry, having a wealth of knowledge to help you. She specialises in helping riders, service-based business owners and coaches unlock their full potential so they can achieve their dreams and shine their light on the world.

AWARDS AND QUALIFICATIONS –

- BHS Accredited Coach
- Awarded UKCC Level 4 at the BHS National Convention *there are currently only 42 equestrian coaches in the UK who hold this qualification.
- BHS Accredited Professional Coach with BHS SC (Stage 5 Coach)
- BHS SM (BHS Stage 5 Care and Management)
- Postgraduate Diploma in Professional Sports Coaching Practice, Level 5 Diploma in Education and Training. An HND in Equine Management.
- First Aid
- Safeguarding course
- Finalist for Coach of the Year in the Northeast Disability Sports Award 2018
- BHS II (Stage 4 Senior Coach in Complete Horsemanship).
- NLP Practitioner, NLP Coaching, Hypnosis and Timeline Therapy®.
- NVQ Assessor and IV (Internal Verifier),
- BHS Ride Safe Assessor and Trainer.

DO YOU WANT HELP WITH YOUR RIDING? OR
EVEN EQUESTRIAN QUALIFICATION TRAINING?

You can work with Claire in person at Swinhoe Farm Riding
Centre in Northumberland or online. Claire works with recre-
ational riders through to competition and career riders in all 3
Olympic disciplines.

Claire is very passionate about inspiring the next generation
of equestrian coaches.

If you are interested in progressing onto Claire's online "Keys
to Coaching course" where Claire will help you get prepared
ready for your coaching assessments, taking you through her
coaching foundations.

Claire also offers online courses for coaches and riders to help
with their mindsets and specialises in helping people overcome their barriers, to help you unlock their full potential.
She is the author of 'Unlock Your Coaching Success" aimed at
supporting people wanting to get into equestrian coaching.

If you would like to be coached by Claire, you can contact her by email: Claire@swinhoefarmridingcentre.co.uk

You can find out more about Claire and follow her here:

www.swinhoefarmridingcentre.co.uk and

www.clairenixonord.com

Facebook:

https://www.facebook.com/swinhoefarmridingcentre/

Instagram:

https://www.instagram.com/swinhoefarmridingcentre/

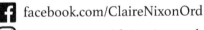 facebook.com/ClaireNixonOrd
instagram.com/clairenixonordcoaching

ABOUT THE AUTHOR

TRACEY COLE

Tracey is one of the UK's leading equestrian-focused NLP and Hypnosis Trainers and Master Coaches. She is a former research scientist, university lecturer and teacher who, since 2013 has taken her career on a new path to spread the word about the powerful benefits of NLP, NLP Coaching, Time Line Therapy® and Hypnosis.

As a keen equestrian and former nervous competitor, it is no surprise that she loves to help riders of all levels combat nerves and ride to the very best of their ability and empower instructors to deliver incredible coaching. She also helps equestrians overcome debilitating mindset problems such as stress, depression, trauma and accidents.

Tracey is also the name behind the Empowered Equestrian™ Coach Training. This totally unique programme delivers riders, coaches and instructors the confidence and focus they need to take their personal performance or business to the next level. The Empowered Equestrian™ Coach Training ensures participants will develop the mindset tools they need to succeed and the skills to be an exceptional equestrian mental coaches, helping others to overcome their personal barriers. She is the author of 'The Confident Rider Mindset – how to hack your mind for riding success.'

Tracey lives in Leek in north Staffordshire and owns two mares, a retired chestnut warmblood and a bay British Sports Horse.

QUALIFICATIONS

- BSc., PhD (University of Liverpool)
- Master Coach of NLP, Time Line Therapy® and Hypnosis
- Accredited trainer of NLP, Time Line Therapy® and Hypnosis

If you would like to be coached by Tracey or to take one of her equestrian NLP training, you can email her (info@tracey-colenlp.com) or visit her website to find out more. (www.traceycolenlp.com).

You can also find her on:

facebook.com/traceycolenlp
instagram.com/traceycolenlp

Printed in Great Britain
by Amazon

34336040R00086